Newark-on-Trent: Bricks, Beams & Banter

Published By Dave Fargher
2025

Keep History Alive

Index

About the Author – Page 8

Preface – Page 11

Introduction: A Town Built to Tell Tales – Page 16

Notes on Grading – Page 18

Grade 1 Buildings

Newark Castle:
The Old Grey Lady with a Thousand Stories – Page 20
St Mary Magdalene
The Tower That Tells Tales – Page 24
Newark Town Hall:
Columns, Councillors, and Kiddey's Creative Spirit – Page 31
The Governor's House:
550 Years of Power, Plots, and Pastries – Page 35

Grade II and II* Buildings (and others)

The Former White Hart Hotel
Saints, Sempstresses, Siege Damage — and a Sculptor's Spirit – 46
Newark's Thinnest House
A Sliver of History Between Stone and Scandal – 46
The Guild Hall
A Wall, a Chapel, and a Whole Lot of History – 49
The Friary
Monks, Muskets, and Molars – 53
40–44 Castlegate
Jetties, Gothic Scrapers, and Yorkshire Sashes – 57
Moot Hall
From Royal Decrees to Flat Whites – 59
The Saracen's Head
Ale, Armies, and Arched Elegance – 63
The Palace Theatre

A Stage Fit for a Queen (or at Least a Prima Ballerina) – 66
Church House
Georgian Grace, Civic Roots, and Mothering Sunday Memories – 69
The Newark Odinist Temple
Where Thor Meets Tudor – 72
The Clinton Arms
Byron's Bed and Gladstone's Gables – 75

The Ossington: Coffee
Conscience, and the Ghost of Temperance Past – 78
Wilson Street Houses
Georgian Swagger, Clerical Shenanigans, and Brick-Laced Bravado – 82
The Gilstrap Centre & Sir William Gilstrap
Newark's Victorian Gem with a Heart of Gold and a Romanesque Arch – 85
37 & 39 Kirkgate
Royal Lodgings and Timber Tales – 89
The Robin Hood Hotel
From Townhouses to Travelodge, via Tankards and Timber – 92
Newark Violin School
Strings, Scandals, and Soundcraft – 96
The Corn Exchange
Commerce, Columns, and Club Nights – 99
Trent Bridge
Newark's Stony Supermodel of the Great North Road – 103
Longstone Bridge
Long and Stoney – 106
Newark Town Lock
The Gateway That Floated Newark's Fortune – 108
The Former WI House / Toll House
Bricks, Bridges, and Bureaucracy – 111
The Prince Rupert
Timber, Troops, and Tankards – 114
The Old Magnus Grammar School
Latin, Legacy, and Latticed Windows – 117
40–44 Carter Gate
Timber, Trade, and Time Travel – 121
The Lock Keeper's Cottage

Bricks, Boats, and the Backbone of the Trent – 123
22 & 24 Kirkgate
Timber, Tithes, and Tudor Tales – 126
The Old Bakery Tea Room
Scones, Spirits, and Surviving Centuries – 129
Handley House
Bricks, Beer, and Boroughs – 132
Sketchley House
From Ale to Automobiles and Back Again -135
The Queen's Head
Timberly Tudorly – 138
(Former) Chauntry House and deer paddock - 141

Former Factories

Trent Navigation Wharf – 145
Castle Brewery – 147
Former Gypsum Grinding Mill – 149
Warwick Brewery – 150
Thorpes Warehouse – 152
Strays Windmill – 154
Nicholsons Factory – 155
Coopers Dressing Gown Factory – 157
Mills Warehouse – 159
Town Wharf Brewery - 161
Former Warwick Maltings – 163

Historic Points of Interest & Additional Mentions

Civil War Statue - 166
The Town Pump - 167
Beaumond Cross – 168
Queen Sconce Statue - 169
Ironmonger Row & The Church Chimney - 170
Lord Byron's Poems - 171
Cannonball Hole & Chain Lane - 172
Cuckstool Wharf & Smeaton's Arches - 173

Romanesque Arch & Fountain Gardens - 174
Otter Park - 175
Jubilee Arch - 176
Millennium Monument - 177
Newark Roundel - 178
Newark Oriel Windows - 179
The Bronze Map of Newark - 180
Newark Coat of Arms - 181
Newark Cemetery - 182
Commonwealth War Graves - 183
Newark Town Bowls Club - 184
Newark's First Telephone Exchange & Alderman Hercules Clay's House - 185
Ossington Chambers - 186
The Arcade - 187
The Old Mount School - 188
The White House - 189
The Old Railway Line - 190

Newark-on-Trent: A Brief History with Extra Sass

Palaeolithic Era - The Original Flintstones - 192
Mesolithic & Neolithic: From Spears to Spades - 193
Bronze Age: Henge Goals - 194
Iron Age: Torcs, Tribes & Toolkits - 195
Roman Period: Pottery, Please - 196
Saxon Period: From Burhs to Bjarn's Gate - 197
Medieval Period: Castles, Kings, and Market Things - 198
Tudor Period: Wool, Wealth & Winking at the Crown - 199
Stuart Period: Stuart Shenanigans - 200
Georgian Period: Grandeur, Growth & Genteel Gossip - 201
The Victorian Era: Industrial Revolution: Steam, Steel, and Stubborn Progress - 202
The 20th Century: Wars, Recovery, and Modern Marvels - 203
21st Century: Newark in the New Millennium: A Town with a Plan (and a Map)(2000–Present) - 204

Notable Historic Sites

MillGate – 206
Ad Pontem – Newark's Roman Service Station – 213
Crococalana – The Roman Town That Time (Almost) Forgot – 216
Margidunum – The Roman Roundabout Before Newark – 219
Queen Sconce – 222
The Battle OF Lincoln Fair: The Battle That Saved England– 226
The Battle of Stoke Field – 229
The Newark Torc – Newark's Golden Halo of Mystery – 232
Twelve Sides of Confusion – The Norton Disney Dodecahedron – 236
The Myth of the Newark Tunnels – 239
The Old Walls and Gates of Newark-on-Trent – 242
St Catherines Well: The Sacred Leprosy Healing Spring and The Legend of the Fair Maid of Newark - 244

1600's Disasters

The Great Flood of 1683: When Newark Got Absolutely Soaked (and Smashed) – 250
Newark and the Plague of 1645 – Newark-on-Trent's darkest hour – 253

Whispers from the other side: Unearthing Newark-on-Trent's Chilling Ghostly Encounters - 256

More Books – 260

A special creative treat – Page 265

Free Guide to Newark On Trent - 274

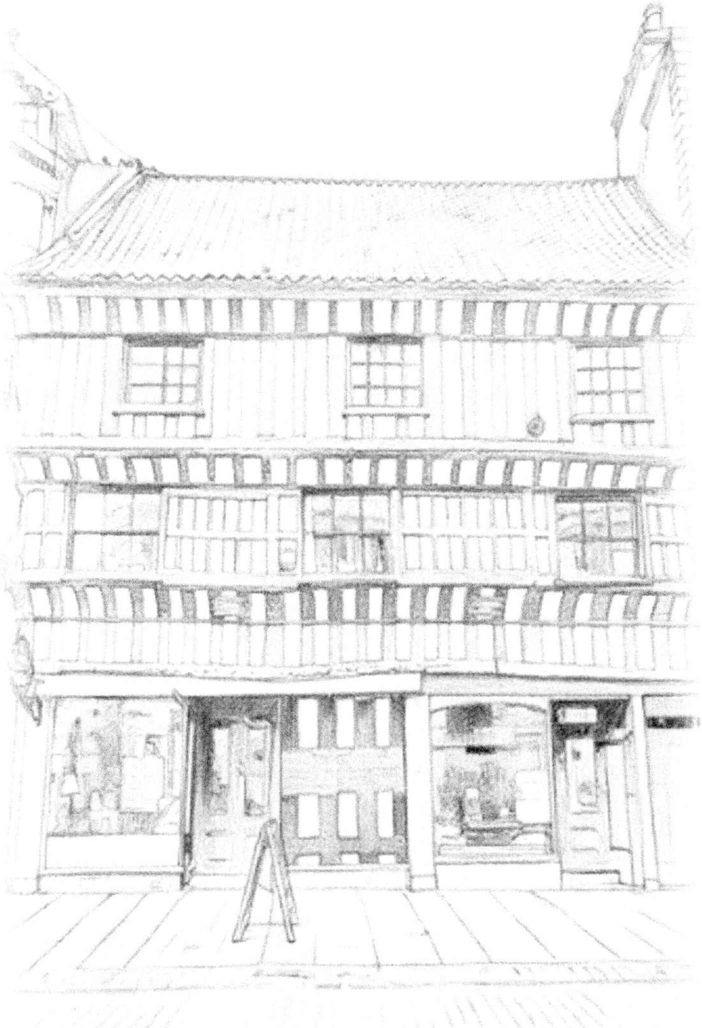

About the Author

Dave Fargher is Newark-on-Trent's unofficial architectural raconteur — a man who can spot a Georgian cornice at fifty paces and tell you what it used to be before it became a vape shop.

Born and raised in Newark, Dave has spent years championing the town's heritage — not just the grand events and famous names, but the bricks, beams, and backstories that make Newark's buildings so endlessly fascinating.

His first book, *Newark-on-Trent: A Sometimes Witty Journey Through Time,* took readers on a lively stroll through the town's history. Now, he's back with a magnifying glass and a sense of humour, turning his attention to the buildings themselves.

In 2021, Dave founded the Newark-on-Trent Photographs Facebook group, which quickly became a thriving digital community. What began as a place to share scenic shots and nostalgic nooks has grown into a living archive of Newark's built environment — part memory lane, part architectural detective agency.

Then came www.newarkguide.co.uk, launched in 2025: a free, interactive treasure trove of Newark's past and present. From pubs that used to be banks (and vice versa), to ghost stories, walking trails, and industrial relics, the site is a love letter to the town's quirks and corners.

Dave also gives talks, supports local heritage groups, and has been known to lead the occasional impromptu walking tour — usually when someone makes the mistake of asking, "What used to be here?"

Whether he's photographing forgotten doorways, unearthing medieval masonry, or explaining why that oddly placed window is a clue to a long-lost staircase, Dave brings Newark's buildings to life with wit, warmth, and a healthy respect for the weird.

When he's not writing or mapping, you'll find him wandering the streets with a camera in one hand and a factoid in the other, ready to tell anyone who'll listen why Newark's buildings aren't just structures — they're storytellers.

His books are designed to accompany and compliment his website; www.newarkguide.co.uk, a free, interactive digital gateway to Newark's past and present. The site includes historic buildings, curiosities, parks, pubs, former breweries, and even the occasional ghost story. It's part history lesson, part treasure hunt, and entirely brilliant

The Newark Guide isn't just a website — it's a love letter to the town. It includes local legends, industrial heritage, walking routes, event listings, and a growing archive of photos and videos. It's been praised by residents, businesses, and tourists alike, and has helped put Newark's quirks and charms firmly on the digital map.

Preface

If walls could talk, Newark-on-Trent would be deafening.

This book is a celebration of the buildings that make Newark not just a town, but a character in its own right. From timber-framed survivors of Tudor tantrums to Georgian grandeur with a touch of gossip, every brick and beam has a story — and I'm here to tell it, with a wink and a warm nod.

You won't find dry architectural jargon here (unless it's absolutely necessary and followed by a joke). What you will find is a journey through the town's built heritage, told with affection, curiosity, and the occasional raised eyebrow.

These buildings have witnessed coronations, confrontations, and more than a few questionable paint choices. They've housed rebels, royals, and regular folk — and they're still standing, which is more than can be said for some of their original tenants.

Whether you're a lifelong Newarker or a curious visitor, I invite you to walk with me through the streets, alleys, and courtyards of this remarkable town. Let's peer into the past, admire the present, and maybe even imagine the future — all through the lens of the buildings that have shaped Newark's soul.

The information in this book has been lovingly cobbled together from a wide range of sources, including archaeological reports, historical records, local archives, museum exhibits, and the occasional dog walk conversation. Every effort has been made to ensure accuracy, and the facts presented are true to the best of the author's knowledge.

That said, this is not a peer-reviewed academic tome. It's a local history book written by a proud amateur with a passion for Newark-on-Trent, a camera in one hand, and a sarcasm dial permanently stuck on "mildly cheeky." The humour throughout is intentional and used to make history more engaging, not to diminish its importance or the people involved.

If you spot a factual error, a typo, or a joke that made you groan audibly—congratulations, you're now part of the historical process. Corrections, suggestions, and compliments (especially the last one) are always welcome.

Thanks to:

Colette, Louis and the rest of the Farghers.

Special Thanks

All the people of Newark, past and present.

Oh, and the Internet for providing a wealth of information and a seemingly endless supply of dog videos.

You helped me procrastinate in style

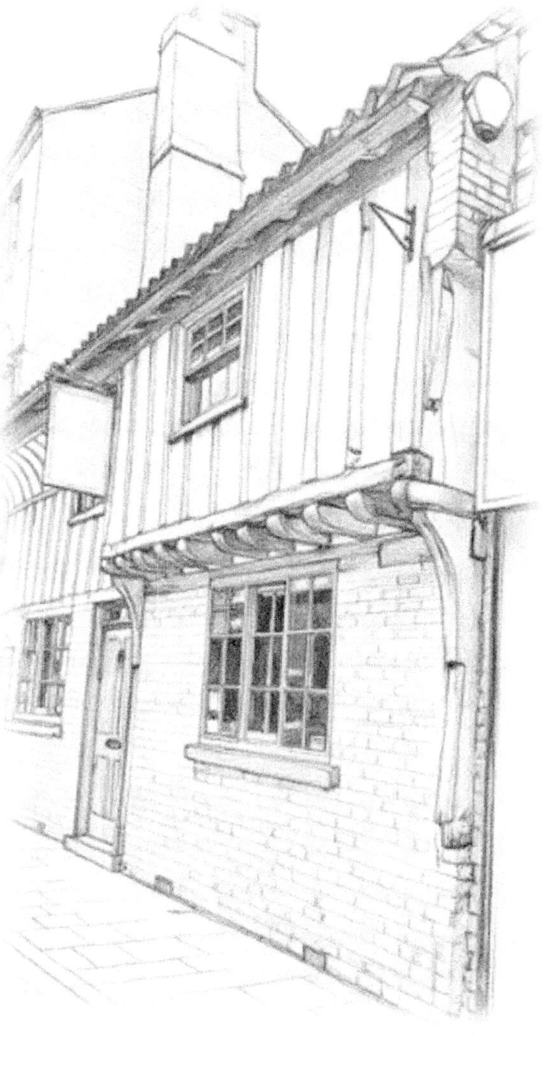

Introduction: A Town Built to Tell Tales

Newark-on-Trent isn't just a town — it's a storyteller. And its buildings? They're the chapters.

From medieval timber frames to Victorian flourishes, Georgian symmetry to post-war pragmatism, Newark's architecture is a patchwork of eras, styles, and stories. Some buildings whisper of quiet domestic life, others shout of civic pride, and a few still mutter about the time they were nearly knocked down to make way for a car park.

This book is not a comprehensive catalogue of every brick and beam in Newark (that would require several volumes, a team of archivists, and a very patient publisher). Instead, it's a curated wander through the town's most characterful structures — those that have stood the test of time, turned heads, sparked curiosity, or simply refused to be ignored.

We'll explore the listed buildings — from the grand Grade I landmarks like the Church of St Mary Magdalene, to the more modest Grade II gems that quietly anchor our streets. But we won't stop there. Some of Newark's most interesting buildings aren't listed at all. They're the ones with faded shop signs, curious carvings, or a story passed down through generations. They're the pubs that used to be banks, the banks that used to be pubs, and the houses that used to be something else entirely.

Newark has over 350 listed buildings, and while we won't cover them all, we'll dip into the ones that have shaped the town's identity. Expect tales of merchant wealth, industrial innovation, religious devotion, and the occasional architectural oddity. We'll look at buildings that have survived sieges, hosted royalty, and witnessed revolutions—both political and plumbing-related.

This isn't a dry architectural survey. It's a celebration of Newark's built heritage, told with wit, warmth, and a healthy dose of curiosity. Because buildings aren't just structures—they're characters. And in Newark, they've got plenty to say.

If you spot a curious structure while wandering the town, I heartily encourage you to do a bit of digging. History is often hiding in plain sight, waiting to be appreciated

So lace up your walking shoes (or settle into your armchair), and let's begin our journey through the bricks and stories of Newark-on-Trent.

The illustrations included are all converted from photos taken by the author. David Fargher

For any places mentioned, you can find more information on www.newarkguide.co.uk

Newark Civic Trust also has a number of walking trails that take in many of the buildings and historic sites in Newark:

http://www.newarkcivictrust.org.uk/town_trails

17

A Few Notes on Grading

Let's start with the grades:

- **Grade I**: These are the architectural Olympians—buildings of *exceptional interest*, sometimes considered internationally important.
Newark has 4

- **Grade II***
These are the silver medallists—*particularly important buildings of more than special interest.*

- **Grade II**: The rest (well over 340)
These are the workhorses of heritage—*nationally important and of special interest.* From timber-framed cottages to Victorian warehouses, they form the backbone of Newark's historic charm

Grade 1 Buildings

The 4 big hitters

Newark Castle: The Old Grey Lady with a Thousand Stories

Castle Gate, Newark

If buildings could talk, Newark Castle would be the town's most dramatic gossip. Perched on the east bank of the River Trent, she's been called the Guardian of the Trent, the Gateway to the North, and—by those who know her best—The Old Grey Lady. And like any grand dame, she's seen it all: bishops with ambition, kings with indigestion, civil wars, sieges, and near-demolition by bureaucracy.

Before Newark Castle was a castle, it was a Saxon fortified manor. But in the wake of William the Conqueror's northern campaign in 1068–69, the Normans got busy. Bishop Robert Bloet of Lincoln built a motte-and-bailey castle here after 1073, complete with earthworks and timber fortifications.

Then came Alexander of Lincoln, Bloet's successor and a man with a flair for grandeur. Known as Alexander the Magnificent, he founded four monasteries, expanded Lincoln Cathedral, and—most importantly—built Newark Castle in stone in the 1130s–40s. He even diverted the Fosse Way to make room for it, with royal permission from King Henry I.

Alexander didn't just build a castle—he built a statement. He added a mint, a bridge across the Trent, and turned Newark into a strategic powerhouse. The castle's symmetrical layout was ahead of its time, foreshadowing courtyard castles of the late 13th century.

In 1216, King John—he of Magna Carta fame and Robin Hood infamy—died at Newark Castle. Tradition says it was from a surfeit of peaches, though dysentery is the more likely culprit. Either way, the castle became the final chapter in one of England's most controversial reigns.

Imagine the scene: a royal feast, a troubled king, and a castle that would forever be linked to his demise. It's the kind of historical footnote that makes tour guides grin and historians sigh.

Fast forward to the English Civil War, and Newark Castle found itself in the thick of it. The town was a Royalist stronghold, loyal to the king, and the castle endured five sieges. Musket ball scars can still be seen on the walls—a stony reminder of the chaos.

In 1646, after the final siege, the castle was slighted—a polite term for "deliberately wrecked." Parliament ordered its destruction to prevent future military use. Only the gatehouse, parts of the curtain wall, and the southwest tower survived.

But the castle wasn't done yet. In 1648, Colonel Thomas Howard tried to lease it as a stone quarry. He was denied. He tried again in 1667. Denied again. The Old Grey Lady had friends in high places—and thankfully, a few preservationists.

In the 1840s, architect Anthony Salvin led a restoration of the castle, preserving its remaining structures. Then in 1889, the Corporation of Newark bought the site and gave it a new lease on life.

Today, the castle is surrounded by Victorian-style gardens, recently refurbished and awarded the Green Flag for excellence. It's a tranquil space where history meets horticulture, and where you can sit on a bench and ponder the fate of kings—or just enjoy your sandwich.

Newark Castle's Romanesque gatehouse is one of the most complete in England. It features massive buttresses, portcullis grooves, and chambers that once housed guards, guests, and gossip.

The river frontage, rebuilt in the late 13th and early 14th centuries, includes hexagonal towers and a curtain wall that once protected the castle from watery invaders. The layout is unusually symmetrical for its time, suggesting a forward-thinking design—or a bishop with OCD.

Excavations in the 1990s revealed parts of the original ramparts and evidence of the Saxon cemetery beneath the castle. It's a reminder that Newark's history runs deep—literally.

Now a Grade I listed building and a Scheduled Monument, Newark Castle is protected by law and cherished by locals.

The Gilstrap Heritage Centre, once located on the grounds, is now the Newark Registration Office. So yes, you can get married in the shadow of a Civil War fortress. Romance and ruin, all in one package.

Newark Castle isn't just a ruin—it's a survivor. It's a place where bishops built, kings died, and soldiers fought. It's been a mint, a manor, a military base, and a municipal treasure. And through it all, it's kept its dignity—and its stories.

So next time you walk along the Trent and see those weathered walls, remember: you're not just looking at stones. You're looking at centuries of ambition, rebellion, restoration, and resilience.

And if you listen closely, you might just hear the echo of a cannon, the clink of a medieval coin, or the ghostly whisper of King John asking for a peach.

St Mary Magdalene – The Tower That Tells Tales

Church Walk, Newark

If Newark-on-Trent were a person, St Mary Magdalene Church would be its memory, its voice, and its best-dressed relative. Towering at 232 feet, the spire doesn't just dominate the skyline—it defines it. It's the tallest parish church tower in Nottinghamshire, and it's been watching over the town for centuries, like a stone sentinel with a flair for drama and a fondness for gossip.

This isn't just a church. It's a layered narrative in limestone, a monument to faith, wealth, war, and weather. It's been rebuilt, restored, bombarded, and beloved. It's hosted monarchs, mourners, musicians, and more than a few pigeons. And through it all, it's remained the architectural anchor of Newark's identity.

The church is a Grade I listed building, and rightly so. It's a masterclass in medieval architecture, showcasing Transitional Norman, Early English, Decorated Gothic, and Perpendicular Gothic styles. But more than that, it's a building with personality—equal parts grandeur and grit.

The earliest known church on this site likely dates back to the Saxon period, though no physical evidence remains. The current building is the third iteration, with the crypt and crossing piers dating to around 1180. These Norman remnants are the bedrock of what would become a Gothic masterpiece.

By 1220, the lower stage of the tower was in place. The spire, added in the early 14th century, is made of Lincolnshire limestone and has become Newark's most iconic silhouette. Legend has it that during the English Civil War, a cannonball struck the spire, leaving a hole that locals still point out with pride. Whether fact or folklore, it's part of the church's mystique.

The church's architectural evolution reads like a slow-motion symphony:

- 12th Century: Crypt and foundational piers
- 13th Century: Tower base and crossing
- 14th Century: Spire and upper tower
- 15th Century: Nave, aisles, clerestory, and chancel
- 16th Century: Transepts, vestry, porches, and chapels

Each addition reflects the tastes, wealth, and ambitions of its era—and the people who built it. The south porch, a two-storey pinnacled structure, is a standout of the Perpendicular period. Inside, the Lady Chapel features an unusually long row of sedilia, and the rood screen and choir stalls (with 26 misericords) are believed to be the work of Thomas Drawswerd of York, a master carver whose work is rare and revered.

In medieval times, Newark was a bustling market town, and its parish church reflected that prosperity. Wealthy wool and cloth merchants funded much of the construction, establishing around twenty chantries—private chapels for prayer and prestige. Only two remain: the Meryng and Markham chapels.

The Markham Monument, dated 1601, is a gilded spectacle of classical columns and carved figures. Nearby lies the Alan Fleming brass, a 14th-century Flemish memorial to a wool merchant. It's one of the largest medieval brasses in England and a testament to Newark's mercantile might.

But it wasn't all commerce and candles. During the Civil War, the church was used as a lookout post. After Newark's surrender, Parliamentarian troops allegedly stabled their horses inside, and the font was damaged—later rebuilt thanks to the charity of Nicholas Ridley.

The church has also hosted riots over churchwarden elections, and in one particularly lively episode, the congregation reportedly locked the doors to prevent the appointment of an unpopular candidate. Democracy, it seems, has always had a dramatic flair in Newark.

One of the church's most haunting features is the Dance of Death painting on the exterior of the Markham Chapel. It shows a skeleton dancing with a wealthy young man—a medieval reminder that death doesn't accept bribes. It's eerie, poignant, and oddly stylish.

Inside, the rood screen and choir stalls are a feast of medieval craftsmanship. The misericords—those small wooden supports hidden beneath the folding seats—are carved with rabbits, grotesques, mythical beasts, and what appears to be a man being chased by a goose. Each one is a miniature story, a flash of humour in a sacred space.

The Magnus Song School, founded in 1532 by Thomas Magnus, is one of the oldest parish church choirs in the country. It survived the Reformation, the Civil War, and the Victorian era, and still sings every Sunday. It's a living legacy of Newark's musical soul.

The church's stained glass is mostly Victorian, including the massive windows in the transepts and east end, installed in 1864 in memory of Prince Albert. But glass hasn't always been kind to St Mary's.

In 1903, a freak storm blew out nearly all the glass on the north side — over 4,000 panes had to be replaced. The Holy Spirit Chapel window was remade in 1957, using fragments of medieval glass salvaged from the wreckage.
Restoration has been a constant theme:

- 1852–56: Sir George Gilbert Scott led a major overhaul, removing box pews and adding a reredos.

- 1937: Sir Ninian Comper added the gilded reredos above the High Altar.

- 1981: The crypt was converted into a Treasury, housing church plate and diocesan artefacts.

Each restoration has respected the church's heritage while preparing it for the future. It's a delicate balance — preserving the past without embalming it.

St Mary Magdalene isn't just a building — it's a living landmark. It's hosted riots, weddings, funerals, concerts, protests, and pancake races. It's been a refuge, a rallying point, and occasionally, a very dramatic backdrop for local gossip. Whether you're admiring its spire from the market square, tracing the Dance of Death, or sipping coffee in its future café, you're part of a story that spans centuries.
And if you listen closely, you might just hear the whisper of a medieval mason, the echo of a choirboy's hymn, or the distant clatter of hooves in the nave.

Special mention story:

"Ringing For Gopher" or "The Gopher Bells"

There is a fascinating and local custom locally called "Ringing for Gopher" or "The Gopher Bells" and anyone who has lived in Newark, or those who have been in the town at dusk in October and early November will have heard them, but you may not know the reason why….

The story dates back over 300 years to a Flemish merchant named Gopher. According to legend, Gopher lost his way on a dark winter night crossing the marshes near Kelham (some say Farndon or Muskham), soon his horse fell into the marshes and began to get stuck (picture Artax and the Swamp of Sadness Scene from Neverending Story - but perhaps not that dramatic) . Fearing that his fate would either be the same or else murdered by robbers, he prayed for help. Miraculously, he heard the bells of St. Mary Magdalene Church ringing in the distance for Evensong. Following the sound, he found his way to safety.

To honor this legend, the bells of St. Mary Magdalene Church are rung on six consecutive Sundays before evensong in October and November. This tradition is known as "Ringing for Gopher." The bells ring from 4 PM to 5 PM, a change from the previous time of 5 PM to 6 PM when evensong started late.

Apparently, with the exception of the Second World War when all bells were silenced, it has been rung ever since the event in question but again there are no clear records. The earliest record is from a parish magazine in 1886:

"Tradition says that a Dutchman, whose name was Gofer, who was chief engineer engaged in the work of draining the land in the neighbourhood of Kelham, happened to be overtaken by fog, and lost in the woods and marshes which then existed there, but hearing the Newark bells he made towards the place whence the sound proceeded, and so got safely out of his difficulty. In gratitude for his deliverance he bequeathed a piece of land, the income derived from which was to be devoted to the payment of the ringers, who were to ring a peal of bells for six Sundays, beginning on the 12th Sunday before Christmas. Though the endowment is now lost, the bells are still rung, and a subscription is made to defray the expenses of ringing."

Local tradition states that he provided money for the annual ringing before Evensong ever since. The date and original benefactor have been disputed over time as any physical evidence has been lost. There are no papers, no benefactor board.

Newark is not unique in having an established annual ringing, often called 'lost in the dark' bells.

This custom is one of several traditional UK customs related to thanksgiving after a lucky escape. It serves as a reminder of the community's gratitude and the importance of helping those in need

In recent years, the first day of the Gopher Bell ringing typically falls on the 12th Sunday before Christmas.

Newark Town Hall: Columns, Councillors, and Kiddey's Creative Spirit

Market Place, Newark

Standing proudly on Market Place, Newark Town Hall is a beacon of Georgian elegance, civic pride, and cultural continuity. Built between 1773 and 1776, it was designed by John Carr of York, one of the most prolific architects of the Georgian era. Carr's portfolio includes stately homes, bridges, and civic buildings across northern England — but Newark's Town Hall is among his finest civic commissions.

Constructed in ashlar stone, the building features:

- A grand portico with four Ionic columns supporting a pediment
- A symmetrical façade with sash windows and rusticated ground floor
- A central clock tower, added later, which has become a local landmark

The Town Hall was built to replace an earlier, more modest structure and to reflect Newark's growing importance as a market town and regional hub. It housed the Council Chamber, Assembly Rooms, and Court Rooms, and quickly became the centre of civic life.

Throughout the 18th and 19th centuries, the Town Hall was the beating heart of Newark's governance. It hosted:

- Council meetings, where local decisions were debated with Georgian decorum
- Public assemblies, including balls, lectures, and political rallies
- Court sessions, with magistrates dispensing justice beneath chandeliers

The Assembly Room, with its high ceilings, ornate plasterwork, and grand mirrors, was the social epicentre of the town. It welcomed everyone from local dignitaries to visiting royalty, and its acoustics were praised by musicians and orators alike.

The building also served as a symbol of civic pride—a place where Newark could show off its prosperity, taste, and commitment to public service.

As the centuries rolled on, the Town Hall adapted to changing times. It witnessed:
- The Reform Acts, which expanded voting rights and reshaped local politics
- The World Wars, during which it served as a coordination centre for civil defence and fundraising
- The post-war boom, which brought new challenges and opportunities to Newark's civic leaders

Despite these changes, the building retained its dignity and purpose. It was refurbished several times, with care taken to preserve its Georgian character while updating its facilities.

In more recent decades, the Town Hall has embraced its role as a cultural centre, housing the Newark Town Hall Museum and Art Gallery. This transformation has allowed the building to showcase Newark's rich history and artistic heritage—including the work of one of its most beloved sons: Robert Kiddey.

Born in 1900 in Nottingham, Robert Kiddey trained at the Nottingham School of Art and served in the First World War before settling in Newark in 1931. He taught at the Technical College for over 50 years, influencing generations of artists and craftspeople.

Kiddey's work is marked by:
- Craftsmanship: He was a master of form, texture, and proportion.
- Character: His subjects ranged from religious figures to industrial workers, always rendered with empathy and wit.

- Place: His art is deeply rooted in Newark's streets, stories, and spirit.

One of his most celebrated pieces, "The Divine Tragedy", a plaster panel in low relief, is housed in the Town Hall Museum and Art Gallery. This work was accepted by the Royal Academy and the Salon des Beaux Arts in Paris, earning Kiddey two rare Mention Honorables

In 2025, Newark launched the Kiddey Trail, a self-guided walking tour across nine locations that reflect key moments in Kiddey's life and career. The trail begins at the Town Hall, where his work is displayed and celebrated

Newark Town Hall isn't just a Georgian masterpiece — it's a canvas for the town's evolving identity. It's where councillors debated, artists created, and citizens gathered. It's where Robert Kiddey's spirit still lingers, in plaster and stone, reminding us that heritage isn't just about preservation — it's about participation.

The Governor's House: 550 Years of Power, Plots, and Pastries

Stodman Street, Newark

In the year 1474, while much of England was still recovering from the Hundred Years' War and preparing for the Wars of the Roses, a wealthy merchant in Newark decided to build a house that would make the neighbours gasp — and possibly squint in envy. The result was what we now call The Governor's House, a Grade I listed timber-framed townhouse that still dominates Stodman Street with unapologetic medieval flair.

The building is a textbook example of late medieval domestic architecture, featuring:

Close-studded timber framing: tightly spaced vertical timbers, a sign of wealth and craftsmanship.

Three jettied storeys: each floor overhangs the one below, a technique that maximised space and showed off structural bravado.

Decorative billeting on the bressumers: carved horizontal beams that say, "I have money, taste, and a good carpenter."

Inside, the first floor was a solar — a private living space for the family, complete with 16th-century painted decoration and vertical sliding shutters. Around 1500, a rear wing was added, featuring a full-height hall, still visible today via the passageway to the left.

This wasn't just a home — it was a statement. A merchant's mansion built to impress, intimidate, and endure.

Fast forward to the English Civil War (1642–1646), and Newark becomes a Royalist stronghold. The Governor's House transforms from merchant's mansion to military headquarters, serving as the base for the town's governors during the sieges of 1643 and 1646.

Its sturdy timber frame and strategic location made it ideal for command and control. It even hosted King Charles I, who stayed here during his visits. Legend has it he used the now-famous long-drop toilet, discovered behind a wall during restoration. Yes, you can sip a cappuccino today in the same building where a king once... well, relieved himself.

One of the most dramatic episodes occurred in 1645, when Charles quarrelled with his nephew Prince Rupert over the surrender of Bristol. Although Rupert was cleared of wrongdoing, his ally Sir Richard Willys was about to be dismissed as Governor of Newark. The tension escalated to the point where swords were allegedly drawn—a royal family spat with real edge.

To spare the Governor's boots from Market Place muck, a diagonal path was laid from the house to the south door of St Mary Magdalene Church. That path still exists today, marked by metal studs—a literal royal shortcut.

After the Civil War, the house saw centuries of changing fortunes. It passed through various owners, survived the odd neglectful century, and was eventually rescued in 1987 by Guy St John Taylor Associates, who restored it with the care of a museum curator and the flair of a heritage-loving wizard.

The restoration was meticulous:

The timber frame was conserved and stabilised.
The long-drop toilet was uncovered and preserved.
The building was adapted for modern use without compromising its historic integrity.

Today, the Governor's House stands as a rare survivor of pre-17th-century domestic architecture in Newark. Its façade is a visual anchor in the town's historic core, and its interior retains much of its original character.

The Governor's House is now home to a family-run café, where you can enjoy a flat white in a room once occupied by kings and colonels. The café is known for its warm welcome, excellent coffee, and homemade cakes that would make even a Roundhead smile.

The newly opened attic event space is also worth a look — perfect for private gatherings, literary salons, or reenacting 17th-century sword fights (though you might want to check the insurance policy first).

Let's get technical. The Governor's House is built using:

Oak timber framing, pegged and jointed with mortise and tenon techniques.
Wattle and daub infill, later replaced or covered with lime plaster.
Jettying, which allowed upper floors to extend beyond the lower ones — useful for space, dramatic effect, and avoiding street taxes.
Chamfered beams, carved bressumers, and coved ceilings, all signs of high-status construction.

The building's layout includes:

A central hall with a rear wing
A solar on the first floor
A service wing with kitchen and storage
A privy chamber (yes, the royal toilet)

Its survival is remarkable. Most timber-framed buildings of this age were lost to fire, redevelopment, or neglect. The Governor's House endured thanks to its robust construction and a few well-timed interventions.

The Governor's House isn't just a building—it's a survivor. It's a place where merchants flaunted their wealth, kings plotted their next move, and architects worked their magic. It's a house that's been lived in, fought over, restored, and reimagined.

And through it all, it's kept its dignity—and its stories.

Grade II and II* Buildings (and others)

The Former White Hart Hotel: Saints, Sempstresses, Siege Damage — and a Sculptor's Spirit

34 Market Place, Newark

Standing proudly at 34 Market Place, the Former White Hart Hotel is one of Newark's most architecturally significant buildings. It's Grade II* listed and described by Pevsner as "one of the paramount examples of late fifteenth-century timber-framed architecture in England".

But this isn't just one building — it's a trio of timbered greatness:

- The front range, built in the 1460s, is a four-bay, three-storey showstopper with close-studded timber framing, jettied storeys, and a façade decorated with plaster saints tucked into canopied niches. These include Saint Anthony of Padua, Saint Michael, and Saint Barbara, repeated like a medieval chorus line.

- The adjacent wing, dating to the 14th century, once housed part of the great hall, later converted into guest bedrooms.

- The rear hall, also 14th century, whispers of banquets, business deals, and possibly a few ghost stories. The building's timber frame includes arch-braced framing, billeted bressumers, and a crown post roof dated to c.1350. It's a masterclass in medieval craftsmanship, with every beam and bracket telling a story of wealth, pride, and survival.

In 1643, during the English Civil War, the White Hart took a direct hit from a grenado (a mortar bomb). Owner Thomas Atkinson petitioned Parliament, claiming the house was in fine shape until:
"Newark was besieged by the Parliament's forces and through a bumball or granado shott... a great part of the said howse was blowne upp and some were there slaine and others mortally wounded."

The damage was severe, but the building survived. It's one of the few timber-framed structures in Newark to bear physical scars from the war — a living monument to the town's turbulent past.

By the 19th century, the White Hart had become a hub of fashion. In 1847, John Cotham Bainbridge — Mayor, draper, and funeral furnisher — turned the top floor into a fashion workshop, employing 59 people, mostly women, as milliners and sempstresses. It was Newark's answer to Paris Fashion Week. Later, the Atter brothers took over, producing Army uniforms during WWI and leasing out shops to high-end retailers. But by the 1960s, the building was in such a sorry state that demolition was seriously considered. Subsidence from 19th-century alterations had left the timber frame sagging like a tired corset.

Enter the Nottingham Building Society, stage right. In 1979–80, they launched a heroic restoration campaign. The building was saved, the saints were spruced up, and the original colours of the façade were rediscovered. It was like giving a medieval supermodel a full makeover — without Botox.

The restoration was led by Guy St John Taylor Associates, who also restored the Governor's House. Their work preserved the building's historic integrity while adapting it for modern use. The south wing, with its coped gable, was restored in 1990, and the rear gallery and stair turret were stabilised and conserved.

Today, the building's three-storey stair turret, glazed galleries, and turned mullions are architectural highlights. The single purlin roof with wind braces, the crown post roof, and the patterned framing in the gable all contribute to its national importance.

So next time you pass by 34 Market Place, take a moment to admire the saints and salute the timber,

Newark's Thinnest House: A Sliver of History Between Stone and Scandal

Market Place, Newark

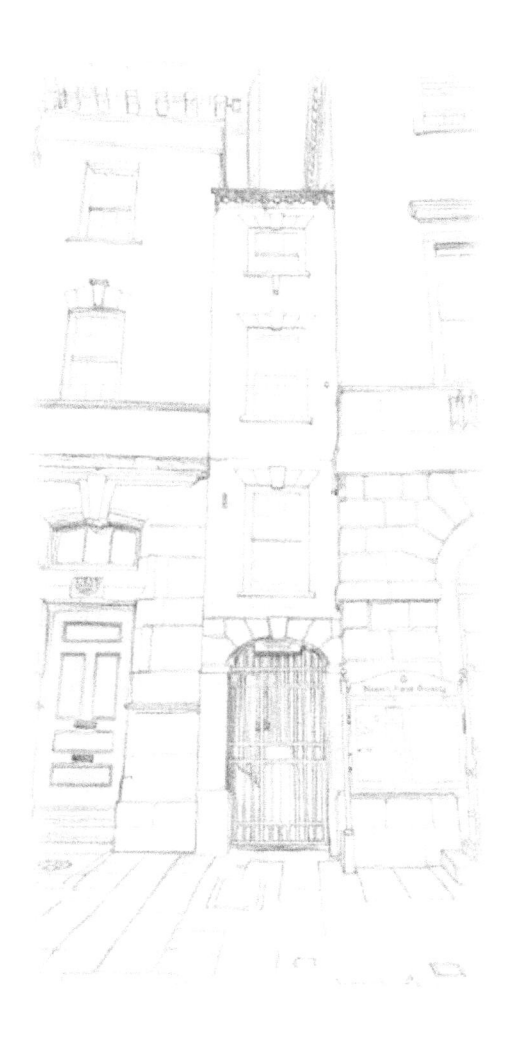

Tucked like a bookmark between the stately Newark Town Hall and the imposing NatWest bank, Newark's Thinnest House — affectionately known as The Little House — is a marvel of architectural minimalism and municipal stubbornness. Measuring just 6 feet 9 inches wide, it's one of the narrowest houses in the UK, and possibly the most charmingly improbable.

Its origins are delightfully mysterious. A pen and ink drawing from 1776, the same year John Carr of York built the central part of the Town Hall, shows the house already standing. This suggests it predates the Town Hall, making it a rare survivor of Newark's Georgian streetscape.

It's believed the house was once part of a row of Georgian shops, including the Green Dragon Pub, which were gradually sacrificed to the expansionist ambitions of the bank and the Town Hall. Somehow, this narrow plot escaped demolition — perhaps out of oversight, perhaps out of sheer defiance.

The story of the Thinnest House is inseparable from the tale of the Green Dragon Pub, which once stood proudly on this site. When the pub was forced to close to allow the final wing of the Town Hall to be built, the landlord was understandably miffed. In protest, he opened a new establishment called the Wing Tavern, a name chosen to ensure no one forgot the trouble caused to him.

It was a classic case of civic progress versus personal pride — and the Thinnest House, caught in the middle, became a symbol of both.

Despite its modest width, the Thinnest House boasts a full three-storey structure. Its internal layout is as quirky as its exterior:

- The first floor includes a sitting room adjacent to the Mayor's Parlour, which has been used for decades as a robing room for the Mayor of Newark, Deputy Mayor, Mace Bearers, and Town Crier before and after civic functions.
- The upper floors are accessed via a staircase from the adjacent townhouse, suggesting it was never truly independent but always part of a larger civic complex.
-

At some point, the house was formally incorporated into the Town Hall complex, likely to serve as accommodation for the hall's keeper — a snug but central posting.

The house's most regal moment came in the 1970s, when Princess Anne, the Princess Royal, visited Newark to open Southfield House on Millgate, a facility for elderly residents. As part of her visit, she stopped by the Thinnest House to collect donations for Save The Children, of which she was president.

In honour of her visit, a toilet was specially installed — because even royalty needs a proper pit stop. It's perhaps the only time in history that a lavatory installation was considered a matter of national importance.

The archway underneath the house once led to stables for the private house and Town Hall. Today, it leads to the Town Council's markets and carparks office, a practical if less romantic use.

A photograph taken before 1902, unearthed by museum volunteer Mr Godfrey Cozens, shows the Thinnest House was once adjacent to a printing firm owned by the Perfect family. The name is fitting — because this little house has survived with perfect timing, dodging demolition and adapting to every civic whim.

Whether you admire it for its narrow defiance, its civic role, or its royal plumbing, the Thinnest House is a reminder that history doesn't always come in grand packages. Sometimes, it's tucked between a bank and a town hall, quietly holding its ground.

The Guild Hall of Newark-on-Trent: A Wall, a Chapel, and a Whole Lot of History

Guildhall Street, Newark

If you've ever wandered down Guildhall Street and spotted a stub of blue lias limestone wall standing like a forgotten punctuation mark in a sentence long since ended — you've just met the last visible whisper of Newark's medieval Guild Hall. It's not much to look at now, but oh, the stories it could tell (if walls could talk and had a flair for civic administration).

The street itself was first recorded in 1302 as Gild Lane, abutting onto Balderton Gate. The name Guildhall Street clings to its medieval roots like ivy on a cloister wall, a quiet reminder of Newark's bustling civic and religious life in the Middle Ages. By 1471, the Guild Hall was described as being "in the middle of Balderton Gate," placing it squarely in the civic heart of the town. It wasn't just a meeting room — it was a centre of power, influence, and community.

In medieval England, guilds were the original G's — part trade union, part religious fraternity, part town council. Newark had both religious and trade guilds, but the Guild of the Holy Trinity was the Beyoncé of the bunch.

This guild was so powerful it had its own chapel in the south transept of St Mary Magdalene Church, and it owned swathes of land in the Barnby Gate and Balderton Gate areas. It was a spiritual and economic force, shaping Newark's development and governance.

Guild members met to discuss trade, charity, and civic matters. They also prayed together, drank together, and occasionally fined each other for stealing herbs from the Guild Hall garden (more on that later).

In 1546, the Guild of the Holy Trinity was dissolved during the Reformation, when Henry VIII decided that religious fraternities were getting a bit too powerful (and wealthy). The town's governance passed to a corporation, and the Moot Hall — now a Starbucks, because of course it is — took over as the centre of civic life.

The Guild Hall itself lingered for a while, used for various civic functions, including as a court and even as one of the town's gaols. In 1594, a record notes:

"The gaoler who keeps the Guild Hall garden shall only give herbs and flowers from the garden to the Alderman's house — or face a fine of 12d for every offence."

That's right — even the parsley had politics.

Today, all that remains of the Guild Hall is a stub of blue lias limestone wall on Guildhall Street. It's not part of the original town wall, but its substantial construction and choice of material suggest it was once part of something important — possibly the Guild Hall itself or at least its boundary. There's also a partial wall in the London Road car park, opposite Pratt & Gelthorpe, which may have belonged to the same property. It's like a historical jigsaw puzzle with most of the pieces missing and no picture on the box.

Back to 1786, when the land was sold to the Methodist Church for the princely sum of £510. According to an 1871 article in the Methodist Messenger, the plot included "the old Guildhall, six cottages, and some adjoining land."

The Methodists used the old building for a while before demolishing it and building a new chapel, which opened on 11 February 1787, with none other than John Wesley himself doing the honours.

This chapel—now known as Wesley House—features a round-arched door, Gothic tracery, and enough ecclesiastical charm to make even the most stoic historian swoon. It was enlarged in 1815, superseded by a new chapel on Barnby Gate in 1846, and then converted into a school, which it remained until around 1980.

The Guild Hall wasn't just a place for guild members to sip ale and argue about wool tariffs. It was a cornerstone of Newark's civic identity—a place of commerce, community, and consequence, where the town's movers and shakers once gathered to shape its destiny.

So next time you walk down Guildhall Street, pause by that lonely wall and imagine the voices of merchants, aldermen, and gaolers echoing through time. You're standing where Newark's civic story began.

The Friary: Monks, Muskets, and Molars

Appletongate, Newark

In 1499, King Henry VII — a monarch known for his cautious politics and fondness for financial stability — decided to flex his spiritual muscles by founding a house for the Observant Friars, a stricter, reform-minded branch of the Franciscans. These weren't your average monks. They were the spiritual equivalent of boot camp recruits: disciplined, devout, and not afraid to challenge authority.

Although the friary was founded in 1499, it likely wasn't fully operational until 1507. Henry VII, ever the generous benefactor, left £200 in his will to support the friars after his death in 1509 — a tidy sum back then, enough to buy a small fleet of sheep or a very fancy hat.

The friary was built on a generous plot of land, with gardens, a churchyard, and cloisters. It was a place of prayer, study, and community service. But the good times didn't last.

In 1534, under the reign of Henry VIII (yes, the one with all the wives), the Observant Friars were suppressed — a polite way of saying they were shut down for being too loyal to the Pope. The site was handed over to the Augustinian Friars, who barely had time to unpack before the entire friary was dissolved in 1539 during the infamous Dissolution of the Monasteries.

By 1543, the land, churchyard, and gardens were granted to Richard Andrewes and Nicholas Temple, marking the end of its religious chapter and the beginning of its transformation into a private estate.

Fast forward to the 17th century, and the site had become a private residence. According to architectural oracle Nikolaus Pevsner, the building's earliest surviving parts date from this period. It was remodeled in 1770, and then again between 1868 and 1877, giving it a patchwork charm that reflects centuries of change.

Today, almost nothing remains of the original friary — just a few architectural whispers embedded in the newer structure. The property is privately owned, so no peeking through the hedges, please.

Between 1642 and 1646, Newark was under siege multiple times during the English Civil War. The Friary Gardens, now a tranquil retreat, were once a key part of the town's defences. The northeast corner of the town's defences — right where the Friary Gardens now sit — was fortified with a multi-phase rampart and external ditch. These weren't just piles of dirt; they were strategic military installations designed to repel Parliamentarian forces.

The rampart still exists as a bank measuring 8 to 14 metres wide and up to 2 metres high, hugging the northern boundary of the gardens and continuing southeast into Friary Road, ending near Magnus Street. The ditch, now buried, once served both as a quarry for rampart material and a defensive moat-like feature. A contemporary plan from the time even shows a bastion — a projecting fortification — jutting out from the northeast corner of the gardens. Archaeological digs in the 1980s confirmed that the medieval precinct wall of the friary was reused as part of the Civil War defences.

In more recent memory, The Friary was home to a dental surgery — a curious twist in the building's long history. It's said that the only thing more terrifying than the Civil War cannon fire was the sound of the drill echoing through those ancient halls.

The Newark Corporation bought the property in 1936 to be used as public health offices, and the dental practice operated for several decades. While the exact dates are elusive, it's a cherished (or perhaps dreaded) part of Newark's living memory.

The juxtaposition of medieval masonry and modern molar maintenance is a perfect example of how history never really goes away — it just changes uniforms.

Today, the Friary and its gardens are a tranquil, leafy spot — albeit one with Scheduled Monument status and a past that includes royal patronage, religious upheaval, and cannon fire. And towering above it all is the London Plane tree (Platanus × hispanica) — a botanical behemoth that never fails to impress. It's such an enormous tree that it's become a local landmark in its own right.

Fun fact: the largest London Plane tree in Nottinghamshire is at Kelham Hall, standing 29 metres tall with a girth of 7.12 metres. That's pretty girthy.

40–44 Castlegate – Jetties, Gothic Scrapers, and Yorkshire Sashes

If buildings could gossip, 40–44 Castlegate would be the trio whispering secrets from the Elizabethan era, chuckling about Victorian renovations, and sighing at modern bow windows.

These three houses, now joined in architectural camaraderie, are a timber-framed testament to Newark's enduring charm.

Built in the late 16th and early 17th centuries, these houses are classic examples of timber-framed construction, with a brick underbuild, rendered first floors, and steeply pitched pantile roofs

The most striking feature? A continuous jettied first floor — a medieval design that allowed upper stories to lean out over the street, offering more space and a better view of the neighbours.

No. 44, the tallest of the trio, sports a coped gable, while the others share gable and ridge stacks like chimneyed siblings. The buildings are arranged in single and two-window ranges, with a delightful mix of Yorkshire sashes, plain sashes, and even a 20th-century replica bow window that tries its best to fit in

The ground floor is a patchwork of doors and windows that tell their own stories. No. 44 features a plank door with a Gothic-headed scraper — a detail so specific it deserves its own fan club. Nearby, you'll find braded shutters, close-boarded doors, and a two-light Yorkshire sash that looks like it's been peering out since Shakespeare's time

These features aren't just decorative — they're clues to the building's evolution. The mid-19th-century refenestration of No. 44 added a touch of Victorian flair, while the rest of the structure retained its Elizabethan soul.

In 1971, 40–44 Castlegate was designated a Grade II listed building, recognising its architectural and historic significance The listing protects its quirky features and ensures that future generations can admire its jettied floors and Gothic scrapers without fear of modernisation.

The buildings are part of a broader tapestry of historic structures along Castlegate, a street that has seen everything from medieval merchants to modern-day meanderers. Their survival is a testament to Newark's commitment to conservation and its appreciation for the oddities of history.

Castlegate itself is a street steeped in history. Once a key route through the town, it's lined with buildings that span centuries — from Georgian townhouses to medieval inns. 40–44 Castlegate stands proudly among them, offering a glimpse into Newark's architectural evolution.

Whether you're admiring the timber frames, counting the sash windows, or wondering what a Gothic scraper actually does, these buildings invite curiosity. They're not just homes — they're historical characters with creaky floorboards and stories to tell.

Moot Hall: From Royal Decrees to Flat Whites

Market Place, Newark

Before Moot Hall, there was the King's Hall—a medieval municipal building that stood proudly on the north side of Newark's Market Place. In 1547, the Bishop of Lincoln handed over ownership of Newark to the Crown, and the building earned its regal name. It was Newark's original centre of governance, where aldermen met, laws were enforced, and the occasional scandal was probably whispered over ale.

By the early 18th century, Newark's civic leaders decided it was time for a glow-up. The King's Hall was showing its age, and the town needed a building that matched its ambition.

Enter Moot Hall, built in 1708—a neoclassical statement of civic pride and architectural elegance.

Moot Hall's design was a masterclass in Georgian symmetry:
- A seven-bay façade faced the Market Place, giving it a stately presence.
- The ground floor featured a colonnade of six Doric columns, allowing markets to operate beneath the building's upper floors.
- Sash windows adorned the first and second floors, while three dormer windows peeked out from the attic.
- The coat of arms of John Holles, Duke of Newcastle (whose seat was at Clumber Park) was affixed to the second floor, adding a noble flourish.

This wasn't just a pretty façade—it was Newark's beating civic heart. Moot Hall hosted manorial courts, quarter sessions, and borough meetings until the Newark Town Hall opened in 1776.

After its civic duties were handed over to the Town Hall, Moot Hall began its second life as a commercial hub. In the late 18th century, it was described as:

"An extensive brick-built dwelling-house and large shop," occupied by Messrs. Fisher and Fillingham, who likely sold everything from haberdashery to horsehair. It was a bustling centre of trade, adapting to the town's evolving needs.

In 1836, the building was purchased by Henry Pelham-Clinton, 4th Duke of Newcastle, and continued its retail journey.

By 1924, it had become home to A. F. Coyne, a radio and music shop that brought the sound of the 20th century to Newark.

By the early 1960s, Moot Hall was in trouble. Structural issues threatened its survival. Enter Currys, the electrical retailer, who bought the building in 1963 and undertook a dramatic restoration.

Contrary to local legend, Moot Hall was not dismantled brick by brick. Instead, it was restored around a modern steel frame, preserving the original façade and roof design. The architect behind this feat was Robert Ingram, who ensured the building retained its historic charm while gaining modern stability. This restoration was a triumph of adaptive reuse—a blend of conservation and innovation that saved one of Newark's most iconic buildings.

Today, Moot Hall is home to a Starbucks, serving flat whites where once quarter sessions were held. It's a curious juxtaposition—modern coffee culture nestled inside a building that once echoed with legal arguments and civic decisions.

The Doric colonnade now shelters takeaway cups instead of market stalls. The sash windows frame laptop screens instead of ledgers. And the coat of arms of the Duke of Newcastle watches over a queue of caffeine-seekers.

It's history with a shot of espresso.

The Saracen's Head – Ale, Armies, and Arched Elegance

Market Place, Newark

If Newark Market Square were a theatre, The Saracen's Head would be the leading actor—charismatic, historic, and always ready for a dramatic entrance. With a history dating back to 1341, this iconic inn has played many roles: coaching stop, royal refuge, literary landmark, and now, a stately shell housing shops and a bank

The original Saracen's Head was established in the 14th century, making it one of Newark's oldest recorded inns. Its name, like many medieval taverns, was likely inspired by the Crusades—"Saracen" being a term for Muslim adversaries, and "Head" suggesting a trophy or symbol of victory. Charming, if a bit gruesome.

By the 18th century, the current building was constructed in 1721, replacing the medieval structure with a more refined Georgian façade. It became the principal coaching inn on the Great North Road, offering weary travellers food, drink, and a bed—plus a piazza of Tuscan columns facing the Market Square, perfect for dramatic arrivals

The Saracen's Head isn't just famous for its architecture—it's got serious historical clout. King Charles I is reputed to have stayed here during his visits to Newark, particularly during the English Civil War, when the town was a Royalist stronghold

It also features in Sir Walter Scott's novel *The Heart of Midlothian*, where the character Jeanie Deans stays at the inn on her journey to London. That's right—this building is not only a historical landmark but a literary one too.

Its 1721 Georgian design includes:

- A piazza of Tuscan columns, giving it a classical elegance.
- A symmetrical façade typical of the period.
- Interior features that may include remnants of earlier structures, including post-medieval pits and features uncovered during archaeological investigations

Though it no longer serves as an inn—it closed its doors in 1956—the Saracen's Head remains a visual anchor in the Market Square, now repurposed for modern use but still whispering tales of its past.

Behind the building lies Saracen's Head Yard, once a bustling hub of stables, servants, and secret rendezvous. Archaeological records show Elizabethan and Stuart-era features, including pits and structural remnants that hint at the inn's long and layered history

The yard also housed other notable inns, such as the Clinton Arms and the Old White Hart, creating a cluster of hospitality that made Newark a vital stop on England's travel network.

The Palace Theatre – A Stage Fit for a Queen (or at Least a Prima Ballerina)

Appleton Gate, Newark

If buildings could talk, the Palace Theatre on Appleton Gate would likely begin with a dramatic flourish, perhaps a trumpet fanfare followed by a velvet curtain sweep. Built in 1920, this Neo-Byzantine beauty has seen more drama than a soap opera marathon, and it's still standing tall—minarets and all.

The Palace Theatre owes its existence to one Emily Blagg, Newark's very own powerhouse of property development. In an era when women were still fighting for the vote, Emily was busy building empires. She'd already opened Newark's first cinema, the Kinema on Baldertongate, in 1913, and developed The Park and Lime Grove. But Emily wasn't one to rest on her laurels—or her bricks.

In 1920, she knocked down the Chauntry House and built the Palace Theatre, a venue so stylish it could have moonlighted as a set for a silent film. Its Neo-Byzantine architecture was the height of exotic fashion: domed pinnacles, Arab-style minarets, and a façade that looked like it had wandered in from Istanbul and decided to stay for tea

Though it opened as a cinema, Emily had the foresight to include a full stage and orchestra pit. She knew the fickle tastes of Newark's public might one day crave live drama over flickering reels. And she was right—within a year, the Palace was hosting live performances, and the silver screen took a back seat to the stage

The Palace quickly became a cultural hub. Its first screening was *King Solomon's Mines*, but it wasn't long before the stage was graced by legends. Sir Donald Wolfit began his career here in 1921, returning later with Margaret Rutherford (yes, Miss Marple herself) and John Clements.

In 1927, the ethereal Anna Pavlova danced across its boards, and by 1950, Cliff Richard had Newark rocking like it was the West End

During WWII, the theatre's towering minarets served a more practical purpose — they became lookout posts for spotting fires. Who knew that architectural flair could double as civil defence?

The Palace has had its share of facelifts. In 1974, it was altered by Gordon Benoy and Partners, and again in 1988 by John Perkins, who reduced seating and added circle slip boxes.

Despite these changes, the theatre retained its charm — an auditorium with balconies on three sides, a flat ceiling of eight delicately moulded panels, and a proscenium arch that looks like it's perpetually ready for a Shakespearean soliloquy. Threats of closure loomed over the years, but Newark's citizens rallied like extras in a feel-good film. Their passion kept the Palace alive, and in 1993, it was rightly designated a Grade II listed building

Today, the Palace Theatre is more than a venue — it's a community cornerstone. It's hosted everyone from Jason Manford to Joan Armatrading, and its pantomimes sell out faster than mince pies at Christmas.

Church House: Georgian Grace, Civic Roots, and Mothering Sunday Memories

Church Walk, Newark

Nestled on Church Walk, facing the green of St Mary Magdalene Church and its stately beech trees, Church House is a textbook example of Georgian architecture—elegant, symmetrical, and quietly confident. Built in the early 18th century, this Grade II listed home straddles the line of Newark's old town ditch, not far from where the East Gate once stood. That gate crossed Bridge Street (then known as Dry Bridge) near today's Birds Bakery—a location that now serves pastries instead of pikes.

The house's location is no accident. It sits on the edge of what was once Newark's defensive boundary, a spot that would have been both practical and prestigious. Georgian builders knew how to pick a plot—and this one offered proximity to the church, the market, and the town's civic heart.

Church House is a prime example of the Georgian architectural style that flourished in Newark during a period of economic boom. The town saw growth in industries like textile tanning, brewing, and engineering, leading to the construction of elegant homes like this one.

The façade is a masterclass in Georgian design:

- Five equal bays, creating a balanced and harmonious frontage
- Chamfered quoin borders, adding depth and definition to the corners
- Tall sash windows, perfectly proportioned and aligned
- Classical columns, framing the entrance and emphasizing symmetry

It's the kind of building that whispers, "I'm important," without shouting. It's refined, restrained, and radiates the quiet confidence of a town on the rise.

Church House isn't just architecturally significant — it's historically poignant. In the early 20th century, it served as a school, and among its pupils was Constance Penswick Smith, the Englishwoman responsible for the reinvigoration of Mothering Sunday in the British Isles during the 1910s and 1920s.

Smith was inspired by the American Mother's Day movement but rooted her campaign in Christian tradition and British history. Her work led to the widespread celebration of Mothering Sunday as we know it today — a blend of religious observance, family reunion, and floral tributes.

That one of Britain's most influential social pioneers was educated within these walls adds a layer of cultural resonance to Church House. It's not just a building — it's a birthplace of ideas.

In recent years, Church House has undergone a sensitive restoration, transitioning from offices to residential use. The work has been widely praised for preserving the building's Georgian resplendence while adapting it for modern living.

The restoration included:
- Repairing and repointing the brickwork
- Restoring the sash windows to their original proportions
- Preserving the internal layout, including period fireplaces and staircases
- Enhancing the garden and frontage, creating a welcoming and historically respectful environment

It's a shining example of how heritage buildings can be lovingly maintained and thoughtfully reused — keeping history alive while meeting contemporary needs.

The Newark Odinist Temple – Where Thor Meets Tudor

Bede House Lane, Newark

In a town known for its Civil War sieges, medieval markets, and Georgian grandeur, you might not expect to find a temple dedicated to Odin. But Newark-on-Trent, ever the town of surprises, proudly hosts England's first and only Odinist temple — and it's housed in a building that's been around since 1556.

The story begins in the reign of Mary I, when local benefactor William Phillipot endowed a set of almshouses for Newark's poor. Alongside them, he built a chapel — a modest, single-cell stone structure designed for quiet Christian worship. With its Tudor-arched doorway, three-light mullioned windows, and timber bellcote, it was the architectural equivalent of a warm hug in cold times.

The chapel served Newark's almshouse residents faithfully for centuries, offering spiritual solace and a place to reflect. But as the almshouses were demolished in the 1980s, the chapel found itself without a congregation — and without a purpose.

After a brief stint as a volunteer centre, the chapel fell into disuse. Enter the Odinist Fellowship, a group dedicated to reviving the ancestral religion of the Angles, Saxons, and Jutes. In a move that would make Thor himself raise an eyebrow, they consecrated the building as a heathen temple on Midsummer's Day 2014 — the first of its kind in England in over a thousand years.

Suddenly, this Tudor chapel was no longer just a relic — it was a living temple, echoing with the names of Odin, Thor, and Freya, and serving a faith that predates Christianity itself.

Despite its new spiritual role, the building retains its Grade II listed status, and its architectural features are lovingly preserved:

- A Tudor-arched doorway on the south side, perfect for dramatic entrances — whether by monks or modern-day heathens.
- Three-light mullioned windows with arched heads and flat tops, restored to their former glory.
- A timber bellcote perched on the west gable like a wooden crown.
- Inside, the roof features two span beams from a 1980s refit, but the original timbers have been dendrochronologically dated to 1554 — older than most modern nations.
-

It's a building that wears its age proudly, like a Viking warrior with a well-earned scar.

So what is Odinism, exactly? It's a polytheistic faith rooted in nature, honour, and the mythic pantheon of Norse gods. Practitioners revere deities like Odin, the all-father; Thor, the thunderer; and Freya, the goddess of love and war. It's a religion that celebrates ancestral heritage and cosmic cycles, and its revival is as much cultural as it is spiritual.

The Newark Odinist Temple is more than a place of worship — it's a symbol of continuity, adaptation, and the enduring power of belief. It bridges the gap between Tudor philanthropy and modern paganism, proving that even the most unexpected buildings can find new life.

The Clinton Arms – Byron's Bed and Gladstone's Gables

Market Place, Newark

If Newark Market Square were a novel, The Clinton Arms would be the chapter with the most footnotes — historical, literary, and architectural. Once a grand coaching inn and now a stately row of shops and offices, this building has seen more illustrious guests than a royal banquet.

The site of the Clinton Arms has worn many names over the centuries. In the 14th and 15th centuries, it was known as the Cardinal's Hat, a nod to ecclesiastical influence. By the 16th century, it had become The King's Arms, reflecting Newark's royal connections. It wasn't until the early 18th century that it took on the name Clinton Arms, likely in honour of the Dukes of Newcastle, whose family name was Clinton

The current building dates from the early 1700s, with mid-19th and late-20th century alterations.

The façade is a Georgian delight:
- Three storeys, seven-window range.
- A seven-bay arcade on the ground floor with Tuscan columns, some heavily rusticated for dramatic effect.
- Gibbs surrounds on the first-floor windows, complete with pseudo-balustrades and pediments.
- 12-pane sash windows on the second floor, framed with moulded surrounds and multiple keystones

The building's symmetry and classical detailing made it a favourite stop for travellers on the Great North Road, offering rest, refreshment, and a touch of grandeur.

Among its most famous guests was Lord Byron, who stayed at the Clinton Arms in 1806 and 1807 while two volumes of his poetry were being printed in Newark
One can imagine the young poet pacing the floor, brooding over rhymes and romantic entanglements.

Later, William Ewart Gladstone, future Prime Minister, also visited — adding political prestige to the building's literary legacy

Though the Clinton Arms ceased operating as a hotel in 1990, the building lives on as Clinton Court, housing a variety of shops and offices. Its parallel rear wings, one brick with a pantile roof and the other rebuilt in the 1970s, flank a yard that once bustled with carriages and stable boys

The west wing retains its dentillated eaves, coped gable, and ridge stacks, while the east wing features elliptical arched carriage openings, now blocked but still hinting at their former purpose.

The Ossington: Coffee, Conscience, and the Ghost of Temperance Past

Beast Market Hill, Newark

On November 10, 1881, a foundation stone was laid on Beastmarket Hill, Newark-on-Trent. Beneath it, a sealed bottle containing coins and an inscription was placed—an act of civic optimism and Victorian flair. This was the birth of the Ossington Coffee Tavern, later known as the Ossington Coffee Palace, a building that would become one of Newark's most distinctive landmarks.

The tavern was the brainchild of Charlotte Viscountess Ossington, widow of Evelyn Denison, the first Viscount Ossington and Speaker of the House of Commons. Lady Ossington funded the building as a gift to the town, with the earnest desire to promote the cause of temperance—a polite Victorian way of saying "please stop drinking so much." The land was purchased from Philip Handley, Esq., for the princely sum of £4,549, and the building itself cost around £12,000 to construct—exclusive of the site. That's a lot of coffee.

Designed by the celebrated architects Ernest George and Harold Peto, the Ossington was built in the Vernacular Revival style, a blend of medieval charm and Victorian confidence. The building is Grade II* listed and features:

- Intricate woodwork, including carved ceilings and cornices by Walker Smith of London
- Pargetted plaster panels encircling the building, depicting the chaos caused by drink interspersed with religious scenes
- A sundial on the south wall with the motto: *"Delay not, time flies"*
- A large hanging sign and fish panels above the side arches—remnants of its 1980s stint as a fish restaurant

The building wasn't just beautiful — it was purposeful. It was designed to lure the town's drinkers away from the pubs and into a space of moral refreshment and social uplift.

The Ossington Coffee Tavern officially opened on November 23, 1882, and it was more than just a place to grab a brew. It was a multi-functional hostelry, offering:

- Ground Floor: General coffee room, boys' room, kitchen, and offices
- First Floor: Assembly rooms for market dinners and large gatherings, a reading room, library, and club room for Masonic and other benefit societies
- Second Floor: Billiard room and dormitories for travellers
- Additional Facilities: Stabling for 30 horses, a cart shed for farmers, a tea garden for summer refreshments, and even a bowling alley

The riverside garden, planted with lime trees, was intended as a German-style Bier Garten — ironically, for outdoor musical entertainment without the beer. It was a place for music, meetings, and moral fibre.

The original title deed even stipulated that some of the profits from Ossington Lodge were to be donated to Newark Hospital — a philanthropic touch that reflected Lady Ossington's vision of civic responsibility.

No good Victorian building is complete without a ghost story, and the Ossington delivers.
A portrait of Viscountess Ossington hung in the Lodge for nearly 100 years. But when the building changed its trade and began to serve alcohol, some claim the ghost of Lady Ossington became offended. The painting was reportedly seen to fly off the wall — a spectral protest against the betrayal of temperance.

Whether you believe in ghosts or not, it's a tale that adds a layer of drama to the building's already colourful history. And it's a reminder that even in death, Lady Ossington was not one to be ignored.

Wilson Street: Georgian Swagger, Clerical Shenanigans, and Brick-Laced Bravado

In the year 1766, Dr Bernard Wilson, vicar of St Mary Magdalene, decided to leave Newark a legacy. Not a sermon, not a statue — no, he went for something far more enduring: real estate. With the kind of ambition usually reserved for Bond villains or property developers, he commissioned two identical terraces, each with sixteen Georgian townhouses, facing each other like polite architectural rivals.

Only the western terrace survives today, the eastern row having been sacrificed to the gods of progress (and possibly poor planning). But what remains is a glorious slice of 18th-century symmetry, a street so Georgian it practically hums harpsichord music when you walk down it.

The surviving houses on Wilson Street are Grade II listed, and rightly so. They're the kind of buildings that make you straighten your posture and consider taking up letter writing. Architectural highlights include:

- Red brick façades with stone dressings that say, "I'm elegant, but I'm not trying too hard."
- Sash windows in perfect vertical alignment — because Georgian architects didn't believe in chaos.
- Rusticated quoins, decorative cornices, and panelled doors with fanlights that practically wink at you. Inside, the homes once boasted:
  - Wooden staircases with turned balusters
- Marble fireplaces for dramatic readings and mild scandal
  - Shuttered windows, many of which were removed during the 1970s, possibly by someone who didn't appreciate the joy of a good creak

Dr Bernard Wilson wasn't just a man of the cloth — he was a man of many cloths, holding multiple church positions and ruffling more than a few ecclesiastical feathers. Pevsner, in his *Buildings of England*, gives him a nod that feels more like a raised eyebrow.

Still, credit where it's due: Wilson Street is a triumph. Whether he built it out of civic pride or clerical ego, the result is a street that has stood the test of time — and looks fabulous doing it.

Over the centuries, Wilson Street has housed:
- Merchants, who appreciated the proximity to the market
- Civil servants, who liked the symmetry
- Artists, who probably lived in the attic and complained about the rent
-

The street has seen Newark grow, change, and occasionally grumble about parking. It's a place where history lives quietly behind brick façades and where every sash window has probably seen something worth gossiping about.

The Gilstrap Centre & Sir William Gilstrap: Newark's Victorian Gem with a Heart of Gold and a Romanesque Arch

Castle Gate, Newark

Nestled within the historic grounds of Newark Castle, the Gilstrap Centre is more than just a pretty Victorian face — it's a time-travelling treasure trove of philanthropy, architecture, and community spirit.

Built in 1882 and opened in 1883, this sandstone-clad beauty was Newark's first free public library, gifted to the town by the benevolent Sir William Gilstrap, a local maltster with a knack for civic generosity

Designed by William Henman of Henman & Beddoes of Birmingham, the Gilstrap Centre is a textbook example of Victorian architectural flair. Think rusticated 'rockfaced' sandstone, ashlar dressings, bay windows, and a terracotta tile roof crowned by a central lantern that practically winks at passers-by. A rear extension added in 1933 and a later porch were both tastefully sympathetic to the original design — because even buildings deserve thoughtful renovations

Originally known as the 'Gilstrap Free Library', it was a beacon of literacy in an era when reading was a luxury. Before its arrival, Newark's libraries were strictly pay-to-read affairs. The Gilstrap Centre changed that, offering free access to books and knowledge for over a century until the library moved to a new glass-fronted building in 1985

One of the centre's most intriguing features is a Romanesque arch, originally discovered in the undercroft of Newark Castle. Thought to be the entrance to a chapel, it was lovingly restored and installed inside the Gilstrap Centre in 2009 by the Friends of Newark Castle. It's now protected under the Scheduled Monument Listing, proving that even ancient stonework can enjoy a second act.

Sir William Gilstrap: Maltster, Mayor, Magnate

Let's raise a pint (of malted ale, naturally) to Sir William Gilstrap, the man behind the building. Not only was he a successful maltster, but he also served as Mayor of Newark in 1888. His legacy lives on in the very walls of the Gilstrap Centre, a monument to his belief in education and civic pride .
If Newark-on-Trent had a civic superhero, it might just be Sir William Gilstrap—a man who turned hops into hope and malt into a monument of learning.

Born in 1816, Gilstrap was the second son of Joseph Gilstrap, Esq. of North Gate, Newark, and Elizabeth Welsh of Hampton, Leake

But it wasn't just his lineage that made him notable—it was what he did with it.

Gilstrap inherited and expanded his father's malting business, transforming it into a national powerhouse by cleverly exploiting the newly burgeoning railway network
His success in the brewing world didn't just earn him wealth— it earned him a title. In 1887, during Queen Victoria's Golden Jubilee, he was made a baronet, becoming Sir William Gilstrap, 1st Baronet of Fornham St. Genevieve

But unlike many Victorian industrialists who hoarded their fortunes like Dickensian dragons, Gilstrap had a philanthropic streak as wide as the River Trent. His crowning civic contribution? The Gilstrap Free Library.

Sir William's family crest, as recorded in Burke's General Armory, is a heraldic tapestry of symbolism: a chevron for protection, escutcheons with galtraps (spiked cavalry deterrents) for military readiness, and a talbot's head for noble hunting lineage
The motto? Candide Secure—"Frankly and fearlessly." A fitting phrase for a man who gave freely and lived boldly.

Sir William passed away in 1896 in Fornham, Suffolk, but his legacy remains deeply rooted in Newark's cultural soil. His name is etched not just in stone above the Gilstrap Centre, but in the town's collective memory as a man who used his success to uplift others.

He was more than a maltster. He was a civic visionary, a Victorian philanthropist, and a man who believed that knowledge should be as freely poured as ale at a market fair.

37 & 39 Kirkgate – Royal Lodgings and Timber Tales

If Newark's buildings were characters in a play, 37 and 39 Kirkgate would be the seasoned veterans—grizzled, glamorous, and full of stories. These two timber-framed houses, now joined in architectural matrimony, have witnessed everything from Elizabethan expansion to Civil War drama.

Originally built as two separate houses, No. 39 (to the west) dates from the late 16th century, while No. 37 (to the east) hails from the early 17th century

Both are box-framed, with jettied upper stories that lean out like curious onlookers over Kirkgate.

No. 39 boasts moulded timbering and even internal wall paintings, suggesting a resident with taste—or at least a flair for decoration

No. 37 features close studding and a crown post roof with no purlins, a rare and elegant structural choice that would make any architectural historian swoon

No. 37 is said to have been the residence of Lady Leake, a local noblewoman with excellent taste in house guests. During the English Civil War, Queen Henrietta Maria, wife of Charles I, stayed here while visiting Newark—a town loyal to the Royalist cause

Imagine the scene: velvet gowns sweeping across timber floors, whispered strategy meetings over candlelight, and perhaps a royal sigh at the lack of decent plumbing. The house became known locally as Queen Henrietta Maria's House, a title that stuck like ivy on old stone.

Modern science has confirmed the building's age with dendrochronology, revealing timbers felled in 1196–1216, 1505–1525, and 1695–1711

That's three distinct phases of construction, each adding a layer of history like geological strata—only with more beams and fewer fossils.

The buildings have undergone 19th and 20th-century alterations, but their core remains intact. They were officially listed as Grade II in 1950, protecting their historic features and ensuring that no one tries to replace the crown post roof with PVC

The Robin Hood Hotel: From Townhouses to Travelodge, via Tankards and Timber

Before it was a hotel or a derelict eyesore, the Robin Hood Hotel began life as three separate townhouses. Architectural evidence suggests the central block dates back to the early 18th century, with a late 18th-century block to the right and early to mid-19th-century additions rounding out the ensemble.

Like many Newark buildings, it's likely that older medieval or post-medieval timber framing was incorporated into the structure—because in Newark, nothing is ever truly demolished, just cleverly recycled.

By the late 18th century, the three houses had been stitched together into a single establishment. The first historical record of the "Robin Hood" as a public house dates to 1781, and by 1790, a survey plan shows the premises occupied by Mrs. Brough and Mrs. Mough, with associated service elements including stables, a brewery, and kitchens. Hospitality was already in full swing.

By 1832, the site was recorded as an inn run by John Allen, and in 1852, it was sold as part of a larger lot that included the Newark Theatre. The Robin Hood was becoming more than a pub—it was a social hub.

A reference to the "Newark Club" within the Robin Hood Inn Yard suggests it was a place where Newark's movers and shakers gathered to drink, dine, and debate. By the 1870s, the site had expanded significantly, incorporating stables, outbuildings, and even a brewery.

The Robin Hood Brewery, owned by John Smith Caparn, operated behind the hotel until 1879, when Caparn moved his brewing operations to the Castle Brewery on Albert Street. The hotel, however, remained a centre of hospitality and local lore.

In the early 20th century, the Robin Hood underwent a major Edwardian remodeling. This included:

- Removal of various 19th-century additions
- Construction of a new two-storey, eleven-bay wing
- Installation of wood panelling and other interior refinements

The result was a building that blended Georgian bones with Edwardian polish—a place that could host both a pint and a piano recital.

After World War II, the hotel expanded again to accommodate more guests. It remained a prominent fixture in Newark's hospitality scene for decades. But by the 1990s, the building was showing its age.

In 1999, the Robin Hood Hotel closed its doors. For the next two decades, it stood empty and decaying—a sad, boarded-up shell in a prime location. It became a blight on a key gateway to Newark town centre, a source of frustration for residents and planners alike.

Redevelopment was complicated. The building was Grade II listed on May 19, 1971, and its location within the Newark Conservation Area, surrounded by other listed buildings, made planning a bureaucratic minefield.

Developers came and went. Proposals were made, withdrawn, revised, and rejected. The building's historic significance clashed with the realities of modern development economics. For years, it seemed the Robin Hood would remain a ghost of Newark's past.

Finally, after years of wrangling, a viable plan emerged. The site was redeveloped, and the new Travelodge officially opened on May 4, 2021. The project preserved key architectural elements of the original hotel while integrating them into a modern structure.

The result is a building that nods to its past while serving the needs of the present. It may no longer serve ale in pewter tankards, but it offers clean sheets, Wi-Fi, and a decent breakfast—proof that even the most storied buildings can find new life.

Newark Violin School: Strings, Scandals, and Soundcraft

Kirk Gate, Newark

Before it became a haven for luthiers, the building that houses the Newark School of Violin Making was a temple of finance. Built between 1886 and 1887, it was originally the Newark branch of the Nottingham and Nottinghamshire Bank, designed by the flamboyant Victorian architect Watson Fothergill.

Fothergill's signature early Italian Gothic style is all over the building: pointed arches, polychromatic brickwork, and a tower that once stood taller than it does today (it was reduced in height in 1957). The bank even included a manager's house, because nothing says "Victorian banking" like living above your spreadsheets.

But in 1891, the bank suffered a scandal when manager Robert James Beard embezzled £25,000 (equivalent to over £3 million today) and then tragically drowned himself in the River Trent.

The bank covered the loss, but the building's reputation was forever tinged with drama.

By the 1970s, the building was surplus to banking requirements. In 1972, it was reborn as the Newark School of Violin Making, part of Lincoln College

The school officially moved into its current home on Kirkgate in 1977, and was opened by none other than Yehudi Menuhin on April 11, 1978

The transformation from bank to violin school was more than architectural—it was philosophical. Where once money changed hands, now wood is carved, strings are tuned, and music is born.

The Newark School of Violin Making quickly gained a reputation as one of the world's leading institutions for violin making and repair. Students come from across the globe to learn the delicate art of crafting bowed string instruments — violins, violas, cellos, and double basses.

The curriculum blends traditional craftsmanship with modern precision, teaching students:
- Wood selection and carving
- Scroll and pegbox shaping
- Varnishing and finishing
- Acoustic tuning and setup

Graduates have gone on to work in prestigious workshops, orchestras, and conservatories around the world. The school's alumni network is a who's who of contemporary luthiers.

Inside, the former banking hall has been transformed into studios and workshops. The manager's house now hosts classrooms and offices. The building's layout — once designed for financial flow — now supports creative flow.

It's a perfect example of adaptive reuse, where history is preserved and repurposed for new generations.

The Corn Exchange: Commerce, Columns, and Club Nights

Castle Gate, Newark

In the mid-19th century, Newark's civic and commercial leaders had a vision: a purpose-built venue where grain merchants could meet, trade, and toast their success. Thus, the Newark Corn Exchange Company was formed, and in 1847, construction began on a building that would become one of the town's most iconic landmarks.

Designed by Henry Duesbury, the Corn Exchange was built in the Italianate style, a fashionable architectural choice that blended classical grandeur with Victorian ambition. The building was constructed in ashlar stone at a cost of £7,100, and officially opened on 27 September 1848.

Its location on Castle Gate, angled slightly off the main line of the street, was chosen deliberately — for maximum visual impact. This was a building meant to be seen, admired, and remembered.

The Corn Exchange's façade is a masterclass in Victorian showmanship:
- A symmetrical frontage of three bays faces Castle Gate.
- A wide set of steps leads up to three round-headed alcoves, each containing a doorway surmounted by a fanlight-shaped carving and coffered panels.
- Short Doric pilasters support architraves with keystones, while the corners boast full-height Corinthian pilasters supporting an entablature, cornice, and balustraded parapet.

At roof level, a central date stone and a square tower are flanked by statues sculpted by John Bell, representing agriculture and commerce. The tower is topped with an octagonal dome and finial, giving the building a silhouette worthy of a civic palace.

Inside, the principal room was the main hall, measuring 83 feet long and 52 feet wide, with galleries at both ends. It was a space designed for business, but also for spectacle.

The Corn Exchange thrived in its early years, serving as a hub for Newark's agricultural economy. But by the late 19th century, the Great Depression of British Agriculture had taken its toll, and the building's original purpose began to fade.
Rather than fall into disuse, the Corn Exchange reinvented itself:

- It became a venue for lectures, exhibitions, and concerts.
- In the years before World War I, it operated as a cinema, showing silent films to captivated audiences.
- During World War II, it hosted performers including comedian Cardew Robinson, bringing laughter to a town under strain.

The building's adaptability became its strength. It was no longer just a place for grain—it was a place for gathering.

In 1971, the Corn Exchange was repurposed as a bingo hall, operated by Silverline, which ran until 1993. Then came its most flamboyant phase: as a nightclub known as Caesar's Palace, from 1994 to 2011.

For a time, the building pulsed with music, lights, and late-night revelry. But after the club closed, the Corn Exchange stood empty, its grandeur fading behind boarded windows and peeling paint.

In 2018, it was listed in the Revive and Survive: Buildings at Risk Catalogue by Save Britain's Heritage, a sobering reminder of how even the grandest buildings can fall into neglect.

In April 2023, after years of negotiation, Newark and Sherwood District Council approved a new premises licence. The building was set to reopen as a nightclub under the brand Club X.

Trent Bridge: Newark's Stony Supermodel of the Great North Road

If bridges could talk, Trent Bridge would probably start with, "I was here before your great-great-great-granddad was born, and I've carried more traffic than your inbox on a Monday morning."

Built in 1775 – Because Timber Was So Last Century
Designed by Thomas Wright, the Duke of Newcastle's go-to architect (and possibly his go-to for dinner parties too), the bridge replaced a 12th-century timber bridge that had a rough time during the Civil Wnd other pretty tough times (thanks Floods). Let's just say cannonballs, water and wood don't mix well.

Wright's version was a stone-and-brick beauty with seven semi-circular arches spanning a proud 51.8 metres (170 feet). The arches and spandrels are stone, but the soffits (the undersides) are brick—because even bridges need a bit of flair underneath.

Between the arches are pilasters, which sound fancy and look even fancier. Below them are cutwaters—stone projections that help the bridge slice through water like a Roman aqueduct with attitude. These now have concrete bases and steel fenders, like a bridge wearing reinforced boots.

In 1846, the railway arrived at Castle Station, and suddenly Trent Bridge was the hottest spot in town. Traffic surged, and in 1848, the bridge got a glow-up: the stone parapets were removed, and cantilevered footways with iron railings were added. These were supported by decorative iron brackets—because if you're going to widen, do it with style.

The new width? A generous 11.6 metres (38 feet), with a roadway of 7.3 metres (24 feet). That's enough room for carts, carriages, and the occasional confused goose.

At the centre span on each side, you'll find decorative lamp standards with panels bearing the Borough Arms and the date MDCCCXLVIII (that's 1848 for those who don't speak Roman numeral). The motto? "DEO FRETUS ERUMPE", which translates to:
"Trust in God and sally forth."

A nod to Newark's Civil War spirit, when trusting in God and charging out was basically the town's weekend hobby.

Trent Bridge is officially Grade II listed, meaning it's protected for its architectural and historical fabulousness. It's not just a bridge — it's a monument to endurance, elegance, and engineering.

If you wander through the underpass from the old Nicholson factory toward the castle, look up and left. You'll see a flood marker showing how high the River Trent rose in 1875. Spoiler: it's *shockingly* high. Enough to make you wonder if Noah had a branch office in Newark.

Longstone Bridge

Off Millgate

The bridge we now know as Longstone Bridge was once The Haling Path Bridge , The old wooden bridge being considered dangerous was replaced by a stone built bridge of 7 arches built in 1819 by the Newark Navigation Company.

Longstone Bridge is an old towpath bridge on the west side of the river about 274m (300 yards) upstream of the Town Lock. The main flow of the river, by-passing the lock, flows under this bridge and then over a weir. As its name implies, it is a long stone bridge, with an overall length of 75m (246 ft) and a width between parapets of 0.9m (3 ft).

It has seven low arches, each with a span of 5.7m (19 ft). It was built by the Newark Navigation Commissioners, replacing a timber bridge that had stood on the same site.
The parapets consist of enormous stone blocks, 0.9m (3 ft) high, with rounded tops.
A curious feature is a distinct dip in the parapets and paving setts in the middle. The bridge is a listed structure, Grade II. Parnham's Flour Mill used to stand on the left bank of the lock approach, just downstream of Longstone Bridge, but it has been completely demolished, and only traces of the foundations remain.

Newark Town Lock: The Gateway That Floated Newark's Fortune

If Newark Castle is the town's crown, then Newark Town Lock is the clasp that held the whole outfit together. Nestled on the non-tidal section of the River Trent, this lock has been quietly managing water levels and boat traffic since the 18th century—like a backstage manager at a very soggy theatre.

Long before lorries and railways, the River Trent was the M1 of medieval England—minus the road rage and service stations. Newark Town Lock emerged as part of a grand plan to make river navigation smoother, safer, and less dependent on divine intervention.

The River Trent, being a bit temperamental, needed taming. So, in the 18th century, engineers rolled up their sleeves (and probably their trousers) to build Newark Town Lock. It was designed to help boats carrying coal, grain, and other goodies glide through Newark like VIPs at a red carpet event.

Constructing a lock isn't just about digging a hole and hoping for the best. Newark Town Lock featured lock gates, water control mechanisms, and enough clever engineering to make Brunel raise an eyebrow.

These gates allowed boats to be lifted or lowered depending on the river's mood swings. It was like an elevator for barges— except powered by water and elbow grease.

As Newark grew around a river crossing, the lock became the town's economic heartbeat. Warehouses popped up like mushrooms after rain, storing goods and making the town a hub of trade. If you were a merchant in the 1800s, Newark Town Lock was your best mate.

During the Industrial Revolution, the lock's importance skyrocketed. Bigger boats, heavier cargo, and more frequent traffic turned the lock into a bustling aquatic junction. It was the Amazon Prime of its day—just slower and with more ducks.

Then came the 20th century, and with it, the railway and road transport. Suddenly, boats weren't the cool kids anymore. Newark Town Lock saw fewer barges and more nostalgia. But like any good historical landmark, it refused to fade quietly. The Canal & River Trust stepped in with restoration efforts: repairing gates, dredging the river, and making the area more accessible. It's now a place where history meets leisure—and where you can learn about hydrodynamics without needing a PhD.

Today, Newark Town Lock is a hotspot for school trips, workshops, and wildlife walks

Kids get to see how locks work, learn about river habitats, and probably ask if they can jump in (answer: no).

There are guided tours, downloadable maps, and even outreach programs for schools that can't make the trip. It's history with hands-on fun—and no homework.

The Former WI House / Toll House: Bricks, Bridges, and Bureaucracy

Next to Trent Bridge, Newark

The Former WI House, perched at the southeast end of Trent Bridge, began life around 1820 as a toll house for the Newark Turnpike Trust—a body responsible for maintaining and improving roads in the area. This was no quaint cottage—it was a checkpoint, a gatekeeper, and a revenue collector rolled into one.

Strategically located to monitor traffic crossing the bridge, the toll house operated under the Turnpike Act of 1663, which allowed for the collection of tolls to fund road maintenance. Travellers paid for the privilege of smoother roads, and the funds helped fuel Newark's economic growth.

Architecturally, the building is a fine example of Georgian design, with:
- Red brick construction and stone dressings
- A slate roof and a large central ridge stack set diagonally
- A rendered plinth, kneelers, and deep eaves on shaped brackets

These features weren't just decorative—they were functional, durable, and designed to withstand the wear and tear of constant traffic and weather. The building's robust design reflected its role as a civic utility, but with a touch of Georgian elegance.

The land on which the toll house stands has deeper roots. It once belonged to Lady Godiva of Coventry and her husband Leofric, Earl of Mercia, as part of the manor of Newark before the Norman Conquest. That's right—beneath the bricks lies a legacy of medieval nobility and mythic generosity. Although the building itself dates to the 19th century, it may incorporate bricks from an earlier house, adding another layer to its architectural ancestry.

Historical records from 1808 mention Widow Brooksby, who paid £3 in rent and collected tolls on the town side of the bridge. She and her daughter lived in the house, making it not just a workplace but a home. A plan of Newark Castle from 1823 shows the tollhouse clearly marked, confirming its importance in the town's infrastructure.

In 1888, the house was sold by Henry Pelham Archibald Douglas, 6th Duke of Newcastle, to Joseph Gilstrap Branston of Winthorpe for £1,000. Later, in 1900, it was sold to William Edward Knight, an agricultural merchant, for £1,500. The property changed hands several times, with notable owners including W. E. Knight Ltd and Ernest Knight.

In the 20th century, the building took on a new identity as the WI House, serving as a base for the Women's Institute and later as public health offices. It became a place of community service, education, and civic engagement—far removed from its toll-collecting origins, but still deeply rooted in Newark's public life.

The building's Grade II listing ensures its preservation, recognising its architectural and historical significance. Though currently disused, it remains a cherished part of Newark's heritage.

The Prince Rupert: Timber, Troops, and Tankards

Stodman Street, Newark

Located on Stodman Street, The Prince Rupert Pub is one of Newark's most historically significant buildings. Originally built in 1452, it was constructed in the Wealden style — a timber-framed architectural form that originated in Kent and was typically reserved for wealthy merchants. The building's original layout included a central hall flanked by two jettied bays, with the upper floors overhanging the street like a Tudor eyebrow raised in permanent curiosity.

The pub's timber frame was revealed during restoration work, confirming its medieval origins and craftsmanship. It's a rare survivor of Newark's 15th-century streetscape, and its higgledy-piggledy charm is part of its enduring appeal.

The Prince Rupert is named after Prince Rupert of the Rhine, a dashing and controversial Royalist commander during the English Civil War. Newark was a key Royalist stronghold, and the pub played a significant role in the town's defence. During the sieges of Newark (1643–1646), the building served as a gathering place for Royalist supporters and reportedly provided accommodation and stabling for Prince Rupert's troops. It was more than a pub — it was a tactical asset, a place where muskets were stacked beside mugs and strategy was discussed over ale.

The pub's connection to Prince Rupert isn't just honorary — it's historical. It stands as a living monument to Newark's wartime resilience and Royalist loyalty.

After centuries of wear, tear, and tankards, The Prince Rupert underwent a major restoration in 2010, led by the Thurlby Group, now part of Knead Pubs. The restoration was meticulous, preserving the building's original timber frame while adapting it for modern hospitality.

The result is a pub that blends medieval architecture with contemporary comfort. It features:
- A terraced beer garden
- A conservatory
- Enchanting dining rooms
- A hidden upstairs venue for private hire

The restoration didn't just save a building — it revived a landmark, turning it into one of Newark's most beloved social hubs.

Today, It's a place where locals and visitors alike come to enjoy good food, great drink, and a generous helping of history. The pub's layout encourages exploration, with each room offering a different vibe — from rustic charm to refined elegance.

The Old Magnus Grammar School: Latin, Legacy, and Latticed Windows

Appleton Gate, Newark

The story of the Old Magnus Grammar School begins in 1529, when Thomas Magnus, Archdeacon of the East Riding and one of Newark's most generous benefactors, founded a school to teach grammar and music. By 1532, the building was completed, standing proudly on Appletongate, just a stone's throw from St Mary Magdalene Church.

Magnus didn't just build a school — he built a legacy. His endowment funded not only the school's staffing and maintenance but also charitable causes across Newark. His will of 1550 allocated income to:

- The grammar school (£270)
- The song school (£105)
- Ten singing boys (£37.16)
- National schools (£150)
- A dispensary (£150)
- Town improvements (£290)
- Church repairs and salaries (£750)

It was a philanthropic masterstroke, ensuring that Newark's youth would be educated, its poor cared for, and its streets lit and paved.

The original school building is now part of the National Civil War Centre, but its architectural features still whisper of its scholarly past. The structure includes:

- Coursed rubble and brick with ashlar dressings
- Timber box framing with rendered nogging
- A plain tile roof and segmental pointed archways
- Cross mullioned windows, raking dormers, and a crow-stepped gable

Above the entrance, a tablet reads:
"This Grammar School was founded by the Revd. Thomas Magnus 1549"

Inside, the main hall features:
- A box-framed overhanging room with arch braces
- A C16 elliptical-headed doorway
- A Tudor arched stone doorcase
- A butt purlin principal rafter roof with arched collars

It's a building that wears its history proudly, from its medieval masonry to its Georgian additions.

In 1817, the Headmaster's House was added, designed by John Sadler Shepherd. It's a handsome Georgian structure with:

- Brick and stone dressings
- A slate roof, plinth, and wooden eaves cornice
- Three storeys, with five window bays and a central pediment
- A moulded doorcase with pilasters and an open pediment on curved brackets

In 1835, the English School was built next door, later raised in 1902 and restored in 1912. It features:

- A hipped pantile roof
- Dentillated eaves
- Segment-headed windows
- An elliptical arched master's alcove with fluted pilasters

Together, these buildings form a campus of learning that spans centuries.

The building on Appleton Gate now houses the Newark Civil War Centre (well worth a visit)

The Magnus Grammar School moved to Earp Avenue in 1909, where it continued to educate generations of Newark's youth. By the 1950s, it had around 450 boys, with 100 in the sixth form. The girls' grammar school, Lilley & Stone, was located on London Road.

40–44 Carter Gate – Timber, Trade, and Time Travel

Carter Gate, Newark

If you stroll down Carter Gate with a keen eye and a touch of imagination, you might just hear the whispers of Elizabethan merchants haggling over wool, or the clink of Victorian teacups in a china shop. At the heart of this historic street stands **40–44 Carter Gate**, a building that's been everything from a home to a shop, and possibly even a time machine — if you squint hard enough.

Built in the **early 17th century**, 40–44 Carter Gate is a **timber-framed survivor** from a time when Newark was still shaking off its medieval cloak and slipping into something more Renaissance. Originally constructed as **three separate dwellings**, the building reflects the architectural style that dominated Newark before brick became fashionable in the late 1600s

Its **rendered façade** hides a skeleton of sturdy timber beams, likely sourced from local forests when Charles I was still arguing with Parliament. The building's layout suggests modest homes for tradespeople — perhaps a tailor, a baker, and a brewer, each with a front room for business and a back room for gossip.

In **1950**, 40–44 Carter Gate was officially recognised for its architectural and historic significance and listed as a **Grade II building**. This status protects its character and ensures that any changes respect its centuries-old bones

The listing notes its **special interest** as a rare surviving example of early timber-framed construction in Newark, a town that has seen everything from Civil War sieges to concrete barges. It's a reminder that history isn't just found in castles and churches — it lives in the everyday buildings that have quietly stood the test of time.

The Lock Keeper's Cottage: Bricks, Boats, and the Backbone of the Trent

Town Lock, Newark

Built in 1773, the Lock Keeper's Cottage stands proudly beside Newark Town Lock, a quiet yet vital witness to centuries of river traffic, trade, and toil. Its purpose was simple but essential: to house the lock keeper, the unsung hero responsible for managing the lock on the River Trent, ensuring the safe passage of boats and maintaining water levels.

Strategically placed on the town side of the lock, the cottage was part of a broader infrastructure that kept Newark's river economy flowing. It was marked clearly on the 1790 Newark map, confirming its early importance in the town's layout

Architecturally, the cottage is a fine example of Georgian design, with:
- Red brick construction and stone dressings
- A pantile roof with gabled and hipped sections
- Three brick gable stacks, adding vertical punctuation to its silhouette
- A plinth, dentillated eaves, and segmental-headed windows

The building's symmetry and simplicity reflect Georgian ideals of proportion and practicality. But it wasn't all smooth sailing. After the flood of 1875, the cottage underwent significant alterations and extensions to repair damage and accommodate the evolving needs of the lock keeper and their family

The role of the lock keeper was more than mechanical—it was communal. He was a guide, a gatekeeper, and sometimes a lifeline for boatmen navigating the Trent. The cottage became a hub of riverside activity, where travellers found assistance, locals exchanged news, and the rhythm of the river set the pace of daily life.

Inside, the cottage was modest but functional:

- Two storeys, with a central door flanked by windows
- A lean-to addition with a canted porch
- A rear wing, also two storeys, with additional living space

Outside, a dwarf brick wall with chamfered stone coping and iron spearhead railings enclosed the property, offering both protection and a touch of civic pride

Today, the Lock Keeper's Cottage is a Grade II listed building, recognised for its architectural and historical significance. Its listing ensures that the structure is protected, preserving its legacy for future generations.

Though no longer used to house a lock keeper, the cottage remains a symbol of Newark's connection to its waterways. It stands as a testament to the town's rich history and the vital role of river transportation in its development.

The cottage is also part of a broader network of historic lock houses in Newark, each with its own story. Together, they form a mosaic of river life, reflecting the town's evolution from medieval port to modern market centre.

22 & 24 Kirkgate – Timber, Tithes, and Tudor Tales

If you were to walk down Kirkgate in the 15th century, you'd be dodging carts, gossiping monks, and the occasional pig. And right there, nestled among the chaos, you'd find 22 and 24 Kirkgate—a pair of timber-framed buildings that have seen more history than a cathedral's confession box.

Built in the late 15th century, these buildings are among Newark's oldest surviving domestic structures. Their timber-framed construction is a classic example of medieval craftsmanship—oak beams, wattle and daub, and a layout that suggests both residential and commercial use

As the centuries rolled on, the buildings adapted to Newark's changing fortunes. During the Tudor and Stuart periods, Kirkgate became a bustling commercial artery. The buildings were likely used as shops with living quarters above, a common arrangement in market towns.

By the Georgian era, Newark was flourishing, and Kirkgate saw a wave of gentrification. The timber-framed façades were often covered with render or brick to keep up with the Joneses—or in this case, the local aldermen. But beneath the surface, the medieval bones remained.

In 1971, 22 and 24 Kirkgate were designated Grade II listed buildings, recognising their architectural and historic significance
The listing notes their timber-framed structure, leaded casement windows, and 19th-century panelled doors—a delightful mishmash of styles that tells the story of centuries of adaptation.

The buildings have retained their charm, with features like slatted ventilators, overlights, and quirky internal layouts that would confuse even the most seasoned estate agent.

Kirkgate itself is steeped in history. Once the route of the Great North Road, it was the lifeline of Newark's trade and travel. The street has seen everything from medieval processions to modern parades, and its buildings—especially 22 and 24—have stood as silent witnesses to it all.

The Old Bakery Tea Room: Scones, Spirits, and Surviving Centuries

Queens Head Court, Newark

Tucked away in Queen's Head Court, just off Newark's bustling Market Place, the Old Bakery Tea Room occupies one of the town's oldest surviving buildings. Dating back to the late 12th century, this medieval timber-framed structure is a rare gem — a survivor of centuries of change, redevelopment, and the occasional ghost story.

The building is one of only three original shops to have survived the sweeping redevelopment of the area in the 1970s, making it a living link to Newark's medieval commercial past. Its exposed beams, leaded windows, and low ceilings whisper of centuries of baking, brewing, and bustling trade.

The building is a classic example of medieval vernacular architecture, featuring:
- Timber framing with visible beams and braces
- Wattle and daub infill, now hidden beneath centuries of plaster and paint
- Leaded casement windows, offering a glimpse into the past
- A steeply pitched roof, typical of Tudor-era construction

Inside, the atmosphere is cozy and characterful. The rooms are small and intimate, with wooden floors, low doorways, and quirky nooks that make every visit feel like stepping into a storybook.
Despite extensive restoration, the building retains much of its original character. Preservation efforts have ensured that its Grade II listed status protects both its structure and its soul.

The building has been used as a bakery for over 100 years, serving the local community with freshly baked goods. Its long history as a bakery adds to its charm and appeal, and the scent of warm scones and fresh tea still lingers in the air.

In its modern incarnation, the Old Bakery Tea Room became a beloved spot for locals and visitors alike. Known for its traditional afternoon teas, homemade cakes, and hearty lunches, it offered a taste of history with every bite.

The meringues and scones were famously large, and customers often got competitive when supplies dwindled at the end of the day. Flowers adorned every table, and the décor celebrated the building's heritage while offering comfort and warmth.

No historic building is complete without a ghost story, and the Old Bakery Tea Room delivers. It's reputed to be haunted by the ghost of a little girl, whose presence has been felt by staff and visitors alike.

Whether you believe in spirits or not, the tale adds an element of intrigue to the building's rich history. It's said that the ghost is friendly — perhaps a former resident or baker's daughter who never quite left her flour-dusted home.

Handley House – Bricks, Beer, and Boroughs

North Gate, Newark

If Newark's buildings were characters in a period drama, Handley House would be the dignified elder statesman—well-dressed, well-connected, and full of stories. Located on Northgate, this Grade II listed building dates back to the late 17th and early 18th centuries, with additions and alterations spanning the late 18th to late 19th century

Handley House was once the residence of William Handley, a prominent Newark merchant, alderman, and three-time mayor. He was also a brewer, partnering with Samuel Sketchley in the mid-18th century to establish one of Newark's most successful brewing enterprises

The house itself reflects Handley's stature: built of brick with stone dressings, it features a hipped slate roof, modillioned eaves, and glazing bar sash windows with flat arches and keystones. The central entrance boasts a rusticated doorcase with a multiple keystone and cornice—perfect for making a mayoral entrance

The building is a textbook example of Georgian domestic architecture, with:

- Two storeys plus attics, five-window range.
- Low-pitched gabled dormers peeking from the roof.
- A segmental bow window on the rear elevation, complete with parapet and triple sashes.
- A four-flight open well staircase inside, with square reeded newels, moulded handrail, and vase-and-stem balusters

The adjoining former house to the left, now part of the same premises, adds further character with its dentillated eaves, reeded wooden doorcase, and segment-headed sash windows.

By the late 19th century, the property had passed through various hands, including a local medic, Dr Ringrose, who likely undertook significant remodelling. The staircase and rear rooms date from around 1880, and the rear elevation was updated with stone mullioned windows

In the 20th century, the building transitioned from residential to commercial use. Today, it serves as architects' offices, a fitting role for a structure that has seen centuries of design evolution.

Sketchley House – From Ale to Automobiles and Back Again

Castle Gate, Newark

If buildings had CVs, Sketchley House would need extra pages. Built in the 1730s, this elegant townhouse on Castlegate has been home to brewers, mayors, medics, and motorcars. It's a building that has worn many hats—and one of them was probably a tricorn.

Though the original owner remains a mystery, by the 1770s, the house was home to Samuel Sketchley, a brewer from Burton-on-Trent who moved to Newark in 1766. He partnered with William Handley to establish what would become one of Newark's most successful brewing enterprises. Sketchley wasn't just a brewer—he was a civic heavyweight, serving as Mayor of Newark in 1778, 1791, and 1804. It was likely during his tenure that the southern rear wing of the house was added, as it appears on the 1790 town map.

The house itself is a fine example of early Georgian architecture:
- Three storeys, with a symmetrical façade.
- Sash windows and stone dressings.
- A once-grand entrance framed by ornamental railings, piers, and gates—later removed and relocated to homes in Kelham Road and Farndon

In the late 19th century, the house was owned by Dr Ringrose, a local medic who undertook significant remodelling. The staircase and rear rooms date from around 1880, and the rear elevation was updated with stone mullioned windows.

Two bay windows were also added to the front façade during this period

By the 1920s, the house had shifted gears—literally. It was sold to Pitchford and Cooper and converted into a garage. The bay windows were removed to make way for vehicle access and a showroom window. The building became known as Castle Motors, and by the 1960s, it had acquired a single-storey extension with folding showroom windows

In the 1970s, the building was taken over by Holden and Son, who used it as a furniture showroom. They began a careful restoration, removing the 1960s extension and reinstating missing sash windows and brickwork. Behind plasterboard, they discovered the original front door, which was repaired, and a new doorcase was created based on old photographs In 1997, Holden and Son completed the restoration by commissioning replica railings, piers, and gates, based on the originals still standing in Farndon. A Conservation Area Partnership grant from the District Council helped fund the project, ensuring that Sketchley House regained its Georgian dignity—with a few modern comforts.

The Queen's Head: Timberly Tudorly

Queens Head Court, off Market Place

Located at 8–9 Market Place, the Queen's Head is one of Newark's older surviving buildings and a striking example of early 16th-century timber-framed architecture. Originally built as a private dwelling, it has stood for over 500 years, watching the town evolve from medieval market hub to modern-day destination.

The building is Grade II listed, first designated in 1950, and its façade is a textbook example of Tudor craftsmanship:

- Close-studded timber framing with arch braces and rendered nogging
- Jettied upper floors supported by curved brackets
- A plain tile roof with sprocketed eaves
- A central canted five-light oriel window, flanked by three-light casements
- Above, a row of smaller continuous casements in a 3:5:3-light configuration

It's a building that doesn't just stand — it poses.

Though it began life as a private residence, the Queen's Head transitioned into a public house sometime in the 18th or 19th century. Its central location made it ideal for serving locals, travellers, and market-goers alike.

The ground floor features a central double door with overlight, flanked by four-light casements. The right gable has two three-light casements on each floor, with the upper ones slightly smaller — adding a touch of asymmetry to the otherwise balanced façade.

Inside, the building retains much of its original character:
- Exposed timber framing, some of it renewed
- Rough-hewn span beams and pole joists

- A single purlin principal rafter roof with collars, wind braces, and arch-braced cambered tie beams

It's a pub with bones — and those bones tell stories.

In 1960, the Queen's Head underwent a significant restoration, preserving its historic features while adapting it for modern use. A mid-20th-century rear addition expanded the space, allowing for more seating and facilities.

The restoration was sympathetic, retaining the building's Tudor identity while ensuring it could continue to serve as a public house. Today, it's a rare example of a medieval domestic building that has survived, adapted, and thrived.

(Former)Chauntry House and deer paddock, Appleton gate Newark

Situated where the Palace theatre is now.

The name "Chantry/Chauntry House" indicates that the original building on this site was constructed in the 14th century to provide accommodation for chantry priests. These priests were associated with the numerous chantries (endowments for saying masses for the souls of the deceased) that existed within Newark.

The Chantry House was situated in Appleton Gate, a street close to both the Grammar School and approximately 100 yards from St. Mary Magdalene Church. This location would have been convenient for the chantry priests in carrying out their duties.

Sometime before the early 20th century, the Chantry House came into the possession of Mr. Samuel Foster of Woodbrough. He significantly reconstructed the house in a Palladian style. This reconstruction was reportedly influenced by his friend and associate, the renowned architect Sir John Vanbrugh.

The rebuilt Chantry House was described by Brown in his "History of Newark" (1904) as "a fine specimen of Queen Anne's reign highly enriched." The principal front of the house was adorned with the armorial bearings of the Foster family. Two undated 19th-century etchings depict it as a large 18th-century building with extensive grounds, which included a deer park. Despite its historical significance and architectural merit, the Chantry House was demolished in 1921.

The Palace Cinema was subsequently built on the site of the former Chantry House.

During or after the demolition, some fragments from a stone ruin on the site (possibly remnants of an earlier structure) were moved to the garden of a property on Hawton Road.

Additionally, a winged cupid tile was found behind the cinema, and carved oak features from the house were removed prior to its demolition in 1919.

A description of the house was given by Thomas A. Blagg (no relation to Emily) in 'A Guide to the Antiquities of Newark and the Churches of Holme and Hawton,' in 1906:-

"The purity of Chauntry House, whose Queen Anne front is sure to please visitors interested in typical examples of this style. The wrought iron gate and railings are also worthy of notice. On the other side of the house is a walled deer paddock of several acres, which for 120 years has contained a herd of deer (though not of continuous descent), an unusual feature in the centre of a town. The house itself contains many rooms of interest. One pure "Adam" in its ornament and mouldings; another "Queen Anne," and so on. These have been filled with a choice collection of eighteenth century furniture by the present occupier of the house, still further increasing its interest to the connoisseur. Being a private residence, this house is not, of course, accessible to the visitor."

Therefore, the Chantry House in Newark-on-Trent was a building with medieval origins, serving as accommodation for chantry priests. It was later significantly rebuilt in a grand Palladian style during the Queen Anne period before being demolished in 1921 to make way for the Palace Cinema. While no physical structure remains, its history is documented in local records and historical accounts.

Former Factories

Trent Navigation Wharf

The Trent Navigation Company was established by an Act of Parliament in 1783 to improve and maintain navigation on the River Trent. The company was responsible for constructing towpaths and other infrastructure to facilitate the movement of goods along the river. Newark, with its strategic location, became a key point for these activities.

The Trent Navigation Wharf in Newark included warehouses and other facilities designed to support the loading and unloading of goods. These structures were built to accommodate the needs of river transport, with robust construction to withstand the demands of industrial use.

The wharf played a crucial role in Newark's economy, serving as a hub for the transportation of goods such as coal, grain, and other commodities. The improvements made by the Trent Navigation Company helped to boost trade and commerce in the region. The wharf was part of a broader network of waterways that connected Newark to other major industrial centers.

Today, the legacy of Trent Navigation Wharf is remembered as part of Newark's rich industrial heritage. While the original structures may no longer be in use, the site remains a point of historical interest, reflecting the town's past as a bustling center of river-based trade.

Castle Brewery

Castle Brewery was established in 1885 by the brewers Caparne & Hankey. The brewery was designed by the renowned architect William Bradford, known for his work on brewery buildings. The brewery's location in Newark was strategic, taking advantage of the town's transportation links and industrial infrastructure.

The brewery complex is a Grade II listed site, reflecting its architectural and historical significance. The buildings were constructed in a French Renaissance style, characterized by ornate detailing and robust brickwork. Notable features include the brewery tower, which remains a prominent landmark in Newark

Castle Brewery played a significant role in Newark's brewing industry. It produced a variety of beers and ales, contributing to the town's reputation for high-quality brewing. The brewery operated successfully for nearly a century, becoming an integral part of the local economy and community.

The brewery ceased operations in 1982. Since then, the site has been redeveloped into a mixed-use complex, including residential and commercial spaces. The redevelopment has preserved many of the original architectural features, maintaining the historical character of the site while adapting it for modern use.

Former Gypsum Grinding Mill

The gypsum grinding mill was established to process gypsum, a mineral used in various industries, including construction and agriculture. Newark's location near significant gypsum deposits made it an ideal site for such a facility.

The mill was designed to accommodate the grinding and processing of gypsum. It featured robust industrial architecture typical of the late 19th and early 20th centuries, with large storage areas and machinery for grinding the mineral into a fine powder. The building's design was functional, focusing on efficiency and durability.

Gypsum processing was an important industry in Newark, contributing to the local economy and providing employment for many residents. The mill played a crucial role in supplying gypsum for various uses, including plaster and fertilizer production. Its operation was integral to the town's industrial landscape.

Warwick Brewery

Warwick Brewery was founded by Samuel Sketchley at the Tower Wharf Brewery in 1766. In 1856, Richard Warwick acquired the brewery, marking the beginning of its significant expansion. The Northgate Brewery, where Warwick Brewery was located, was built in 1871.

The brewery complex included several notable buildings, such as the Northgate Brewery Office Range and Brewhouse, which are listed on the Historic England website. The architecture of these buildings reflects the industrial style of the late 19th century, with robust brickwork and functional design elements suited to brewing operations.

Warwick Brewery played a crucial role in Newark's brewing industry. In 1888, the brewery merged with Richardson, Earp & Slater's Trent Brewery to form Warwicks and Richardson's Ltd. This merger allowed the company to expand its operations and increase its market presence. The brewery produced a variety of beers and ales, which were distributed widely.

In 1962, Warwick Brewery was acquired by John Smith's Tadcaster Brewery Co. Ltd., and brewing operations ceased in 1966. Despite the closure, many of the original buildings remain standing and have been repurposed for residential and commercial use. The brewery's legacy continues to be remembered as an integral part of Newark's industrial heritage.

Thorpes Warehouse

Thorpe's Warehouse, located on Millgate, was built in 1872 as a riverside barley store and malt house. Its strategic location along the River Trent facilitated the transportation of goods, making it an important part of Newark's industrial landscape. The warehouse is a Grade II listed building, reflecting its architectural and historical significance. The structure features traditional 19th-century industrial design elements, including robust brickwork and large storage spaces. The east-facing elevation of the building is particularly notable for its historical character.

In 1932, the premises were acquired by Newark Egg Packers Ltd., and the building was converted from a malt house to a warehouse. This transition marked a new phase in its use, adapting to the changing industrial needs of the area. Later, in the 1980s or early 1990s, the building was rented out to Weston Mill Pottery.

The warehouse lay vacant between 2007 and 2010 until planning permission was granted in 2011 for its restoration and conversion into high-quality commercial suites and residential apartments. The project was completed around 2013 or 2014, with the original hand-painted inscription "Thorpe's Warehouse" restored. Today, it comprises 12 luxury apartments, blending modern living with historical charm.

Strays Windmill

Stray's Windmill was first recorded on maps in 1825. It was one of several windmills in the Newark area, reflecting the town's agricultural heritage. Windmills were essential for grinding grain into flour, a crucial process for local food production.

The windmill was a traditional tower mill, a common design in the 19th century. Tower mills are characterized by their tall, cylindrical structures made of brick or stone, with a rotating cap that allows the sails to turn into the wind. Stray's Windmill would have featured these typical elements, although specific architectural details are less documented.

Located between Newark and Farndon

Nicholsons Factory

Nicholson's factories in Newark-on-Trent, particularly the Trent Ironworks, have a storied history that reflects the town's industrial heritage.

Nicholson's Iron Foundry was established by Benjamin Nicholson, who was born in South Carlton near Lincoln in 1785. By 1809, he had moved to Newark and started trading as a partner in Nicholson, Bemrose & Co., retail ironmongers. In 1820, he entered the wholesale iron business, and by 1825, he had opened a foundry for manufacturing cast-iron domestic goods.

The Trent Ironworks, located along the River Trent, was ideally situated for industrial operations. The site included a wharf beside the river and sidings onto the Midland Railway's Nottingham to Lincoln line, facilitating the efficient receipt of raw materials and dispatch of finished products. The foundry's distinctive clock-tower, which housed the drawing offices, managers' offices, and clerks' department, remains a prominent landmark in Newark.

Coopers Dressing Gown Factory

Cooper's Dressing Gown Factory was established in 1894 on Victoria Street. The factory was known for producing a wide range of garments, but it became particularly famous for its quilted dressing gowns. The business originally started with the production of workmen's shirts in the early 19th century by the owner of Freeman's Drapery Warehouse. As demand grew, the factory expanded its product line to include women's wear such as tea gowns and underclothes, styled to the latest French designs.

The factory was purpose-built to accommodate the growing business. It featured modern facilities for the time and was designed to maximize production efficiency. The building's architecture reflected the industrial style of the late 19th century, with functional design elements suited to garment manufacturing.

Victoria Street, Newark

Mills Warehouse

Mills Warehouse in Newark-on-Trent is a historic building located along the River Trent. Originally a 19th-century industrial mill, it has recently been the focus of redevelopment efforts to transform it into residential apartments.

The warehouse played a significant role in Newark's industrial past, contributing to the town's economic growth during the 19th century. Its location by the river was strategic for transporting goods

Town Wharf Brewery

The Town Wharf Brewery, originally known as Handley and Sketchley's Town Wharf Brewery, was established around 1766. Samuel Sketchley, who learned his craft in Burton-on-Trent, partnered with William Handley, a local banker. This partnership marked the beginning of large-scale commercial brewing in Newark.

The brewery was strategically located near the River Trent, which was crucial for transporting goods. The site included warehouses and wharves, allowing for efficient distribution of ale

The building's design was influenced by its function as a transport interchange, facilitating the movement of goods by both land and water

The Wharf, Newark

Former Warwick Maltings

The former Warwick Maltings in Newark-on-Trent, also known as the Warwick and Richardson's Brewery malt house, is a significant historical building with a rich past.

The malt house was constructed in 1864 by Warwick and Richardson's Brewery. The building was made using bricks from the Cafferata company at Beacon Hill and ironwork supplied by the Trent Ironworks of W.N. Nicholson & Sons. This construction reflects the industrial growth and architectural style of the period.

The malt house is a three-storey building with a basement, built of red brick with yellow brick dressings. It features gabled and hipped slate roofs, which are characteristic of the industrial architecture of the 19th century. The building's design includes a date stone on the northeast gable inscribed with "P W Archt. 1864"

Historic Points of Interest & Additional Mentions

Civil War Statue

Located outside the Ossington, the Civil War statue is a prominent monument that commemorates Newark's significant role during the English Civil War. The statue depicts a Royalist soldier, symbolizing the town's steadfast loyalty to King Charles I during the three sieges between 1643 and 1646. Erected in 1988, and moved to its current location recently, the statue serves as a reminder of Newark's turbulent past and its strategic importance during one of England's most tumultuous periods.

The Town Pump

The Newark Town Pump, situated in the Market Place, is a historic landmark dating back to the 18th century. Originally installed to provide a reliable source of clean water for the town's residents, the cast-iron pump features ornate detailing typical of the period's craftsmanship. Although no longer in use, the town pump remains a cherished part of Newark's historical landscape, reflecting the town's development and the importance of public utilities in urban life.

Beaumond Cross

Beaumond Cross, located in the Library Gardens, is a historic monument with a rich history dating back to the medieval period. Believed to have been erected in the late 13th or early 14th century during the reign of Edward III, the cross is a fine example of Edwardian English Gothic architecture. Despite weathering and the passage of time, the Beaumond Cross remains a well-preserved and significant landmark in Newark, reflecting the town's medieval heritage and architectural history.

Queen Sconce Statue

The Civil War statue on Queen's Sconce in Sconce Park is a notable monument commemorating Newark's role during the English Civil War. The statue, a latticework cannon, honors the Royalist forces who defended Newark during the sieges from 1643 to 1646. The Queen's Sconce itself is a well-preserved earthwork fortification named after Queen Henrietta Maria, the wife of King Charles I. This site serves as an educational and historical landmark, attracting visitors interested in Newark's Civil War heritage.

Ironmonger Row & The Church Chimney

Ironmonger Row is a historic street that reflects Newark's rich commercial heritage. Once home to numerous ironmongers and related trades, the street is lined with buildings showcasing a mix of architectural styles. The church chimney near St. Mary Magdalene Church, built in 1854, served the church's heating boiler. Preserved by the Newark Local History Society, the chimney reflects its significance as part of the church's infrastructure and the broader historical landscape of Newark.

Lord Byron's Poems

A plaque commemorating Lord Byron's poems is located on the outside of G.H. Porters at the corner of Market Place and Ridge Street. It marks the spot where S. and J. Ridge, a local printing firm, published Byron's first volumes of poetry, "Fugitive Pieces" in November 1806 and "Hours of Idleness" in July 1807. This plaque highlights Newark's connection to the famous Romantic poet and celebrates the town's literary heritage.

Cannonball Hole

The cannonball hole in the spire of St. Mary Magdalene Church is a poignant reminder of Newark's turbulent history during the English Civil War. The church tower served as a lookout point for the Royalist garrison during the sieges of Newark. In 1644, a Parliamentarian cannonball struck the spire, leaving a visible hole that remains to this day. This historical scar is part of the Civil War Trail in Newark, highlighting the town's strategic importance and the fierce battles that took place there.

Chain Lane

Chain Lane is a historic street that reflects Newark's rich architectural and commercial heritage. Home to several Grade II listed buildings dating back to the 18th and 19th centuries, the lane showcases traditional brick construction and period architectural details. Chain Lane has long been a part of Newark's bustling town center, blending historical charm with modern amenities.

Cuckstool Wharf

Cuckstool Wharf, located along Castle Gate, dates back to the Stuart period and was used extensively during the Victorian era. The wharf served as a key point for loading and unloading goods transported via the River Trent, contributing significantly to Newark's commercial activity. Although now disused, Cuckstool Wharf remains an important part of the town's industrial heritage.

Smeaton's Arches

At the riverside arena, the site that the cattle market was relocated to in 1885. At the far side, at the foot of the wall, can be seen the tops of seven arches.

These are the remains of some of Smeaton's Arches. In 1772, John Smeaton FRS, was commissioned to create a viaduct from Muskham Bridge to Newark Trent Bridge to allow winter passage across the flood plain for the lucrative coach traffic on the Great North Road.

The arches you see are in fact 16ft 6in (5m) tall from top to (underground) bottom and are set on brick piers 16ft 6in (5m) between centres; they were filled in when the ground level was raised as a flood control measure in 1932. Eighty five of the original 105 arches still exist and some may be seen beyond the A46 roundabout, still performing their original role whenever the Trent floods.
The design is robust, elegant, and unmistakably Smeaton-esque: practical, durable, and quietly brilliant

Romanesque Arch

The Romanesque Arch, located in the Gilstrap Centre, is an elaborately carved structure believed to have been the entrance to a chapel within Newark Castle. Erected by the Friends of Newark Castle in 2009, the arch is thought to have been unearthed in the Castle Grounds or recovered from the river. It lay in the Castle undercroft for some 50 years before being restored and displayed.

Fountain Gardens

Fountain Gardens, a charming public park dating back to the Victorian era, features a central fountain, well-maintained flower beds, pathways, and seating areas. The gardens provide a tranquil green space for residents and visitors, reflecting Newark's commitment to preserving its historical and recreational spaces.

Otter Park

Otter Park, a small public park located on Millgate, features a central sculpture of two bronze otters created by artist Judith Bluck around 2009-2010. The park offers a peaceful green space for residents and visitors, forming part of Newark's Riverside Walk.

Jubilee Arch

Commissioned by the town council to mark the Queen's Golden Jubilee in 2002, the Jubilee Arch stands as a testament to Newark's celebration of significant national events. Located in the Library Gardens

Millennium Monument

The Millennium Monument, unveiled in 2000 to mark the turn of the millennium, is a striking sculpture located in the riverside park. The monument features a contemporary design with a central column surrounded by smaller plaques representing different aspects of Newark's history.

Newark Roundel

The Newark Roundel, a distinctive circular plaque located outside St. Mary Magdalene Church, commemorates the different Newarks of the world

Newark Oriel Windows

Newark is home to a surprising number of oriel windows, a form of bay window that protrudes from the main wall of a building but does not reach the ground. Supported by corbels or brackets, oriel windows are commonly found projecting from upper floors and are a notable feature of the town's architectural heritage.

The Bronze Map of Newark

The bronze map of Newark, located in the Castle Grounds, is a detailed, tactile representation of the town's historical layout. Installed as part of the town's heritage trail, the map highlights significant sites such as Newark Castle, the Church of St. Mary Magdalene, and the Market Square.

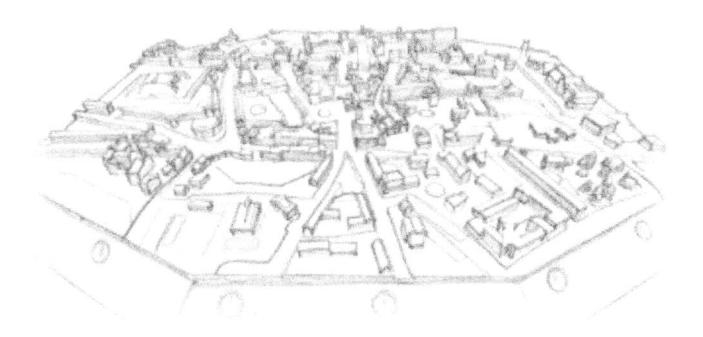

Newark Coat of Arms

Granted on December 8, 1561, the Newark Coat of Arms features wavy bars, a crest, and supporters (an otter and a beaver) that refer to Newark's riverside position. The motto, "DEO FRETUS ERUMPE" (Trust God, and sally forth), is a translation of the valiant words of the Mayor during the siege of Newark by the Parliamentarians in 1646.

Newark Cemetery

Established in 1856, Newark Cemetery on London Road features grounds, buildings, and an entrance lodge. The cemetery serves as a place of reflection and remembrance, with sections for the Church of England, Dissenters, and Roman Catholics.

Commonwealth War Graves

Newark Cemetery is home to a significant number of Commonwealth war graves, reflecting the area's historical military importance. The cemetery contains 49 burials from the First World War and a special plot for RAF burials during the Second World War, including 90 Commonwealth burials and 397 Polish burials.

Newark Town Bowls Club

The Newark Town Bowls Club, established in 1809, is the oldest bowling club in Nottinghamshire. The former clubhouse features a richly ornamented Regency Gothic pediment and an elegant balcony, with an inscription under the balcony reading, "Let no man be biased."

Newark's First Telephone Exchange

Newark's first telephone exchange, built by the National Telephone Company, opened on Portland Street in 1895. The exchange marked the beginning of modern telecommunications in the town.

Alderman Hercules Clay's House

The site of Hercules Clay's House, the Mayor of Newark during the Civil War, is located in the Market Place. Clay had several premonitions of his house being destroyed and moved his family to a safer location just in time.

Ossington Chambers

Ossington Chambers, a terrace of four large houses with steep-pitched roofs, is now used as offices. Built in the 17th-century style, the houses were formerly known as Castle Terrace.

The Arcade

Built in 1897 by the Atter brothers, The Arcade became a fashionable shopping place in Newark. The curved window at the Market Place end was once part of Stanley Noble's small bakery shop known as "Pie Corner".

The Old Mount School

The Old Mount School, with its tower dating from 1877, is a Grade II listed building that has been refurbished as part of a redevelopment project. The schoolroom dates from 1826, and the cross wing to the left of the tower from 1838.

The White House

The White House on Millgate, a substantial mansion dating from the mid-18th century, was once home to Thomas Earp, a maltster, mayor, and Liberal MP for Newark. The house features elaborate Georgian-style internal fittings and a walled garden stretching down to the river.

The Old Railway Line

The Newark to Bottesford railway, open to passenger traffic between 1878 and 1955, offered a route to Nottingham and Leicester. The line is now open to cyclists and pedestrians, providing picturesque views and a peaceful scenic ride between Newark and Cotham.

Newark-on-Trent: A Brief History with Extra Sass:

Condensed TimeLine

To see a full and detailed (and somewhat humorous) History of Newark, the other book in this series is for you:

Newark On Trent: A Sometimes Witty Journey Through Time

is available in my shop
www.newarkguide.co.uk/shop

1. Palaeolithic Era - The Original Flintstones

(c. 14,000BC – c. 10,000 BC)

Long before Newark had a name, it was a magnet for prehistoric life thanks to its rich flint deposits and strategic location by the River Trent. Around 14,000 years ago, early humans—Team Prehistoric—set up seasonal camps at Farndon Fields, drawn by the abundance of wild horses and red deer migrating through what was essentially the M25 of the Ice Age. Between 1991 and 2018, the Farndon Archaeological Research Institute unearthed a remarkable collection of flint tools—scrapers, blades, and points—suggesting that Newark served as a recurring stopover for nomadic groups over thousands of years, a kind of prehistoric Airbnb for hunter-gatherers.

2. Mesolithic & Neolithic: From Spears to Spades. (c. 10,000BC – c. 3300 BC)

As the Ice Age thawed, Mesolithic communities arrived with microliths—tiny flint tools mounted on wood to create arrows—marking a shift from roaming hunters to semi-settled foragers. Newark's archaeological record is sparse for this period, but the gradual transition to Neolithic life is evident in the emergence of farming, forest clearing, and the creation of early field systems. Polished stone axes and pottery shards from this era show a growing sophistication, and the reuse of a Neolithic axe as a whetstone hints at a culture that valued practicality and sustainability long before it was trendy.

3. Bronze Age: Henge Goals
(c. 3300 BC – c. 700 BC)

In 2016–2017, archaeologists uncovered a Bronze Age henge monument at Middlebeck, complete with a circular ditch, upright timbers, and a raised causeway — likely used for ceremonies or gatherings near a natural spring. This site also yielded urns, necklace beads, and a polished stone axe from Langdale, Cumbria, buried alongside Iron Age pottery, suggesting these items were treasured heirlooms passed down through generations. The discovery of 35 cremation burials and evidence of a thriving Iron Age farming community underscores the area's long-standing significance and the evolution of its cultural practices.

4. Iron Age: Torcs, Tribes & Toolkits
(c. 800 BC – c. 43 AD)

During the Iron Age, Newark was part of the Corieltauvi tribe's territory, a largely agrarian society with its capital at modern-day Leicester. Archaeological finds east of Bow Bridge Lane include roundhouses, pottery, and a Neolithic axe repurposed as a whetstone, showcasing a culture of reuse. The Newark Civil War Museum houses Iron Age artifacts like a bone weaving comb, dagger fragments, and a loom weight, but the star attraction is the Newark Torc—a stunning gold neck ornament dated between 250–50 BC, discovered in 2005 by a metal detectorist and hailed as a masterpiece of Iron Age craftsmanship.

5. Roman Period: Pottery, Please
(43 AD – 410 AD)

Although Newark didn't earn a Roman name, its location between the Fosse Way and the River Trent made it a vital waypoint. Roman-era finds along Northgate and at Middlebeck include 73 remarkably preserved pottery kilns, revealing a major industrial hub that reshaped our understanding of Roman manufacturing in the Midlands. While nearby towns like Margidunum and Ad Pontem were officially recognized, Newark's archaeological footprint — complete with villas, artifacts, and the standout Norton Disney dodecahedron — proves it was far from a backwater in Roman Britain.

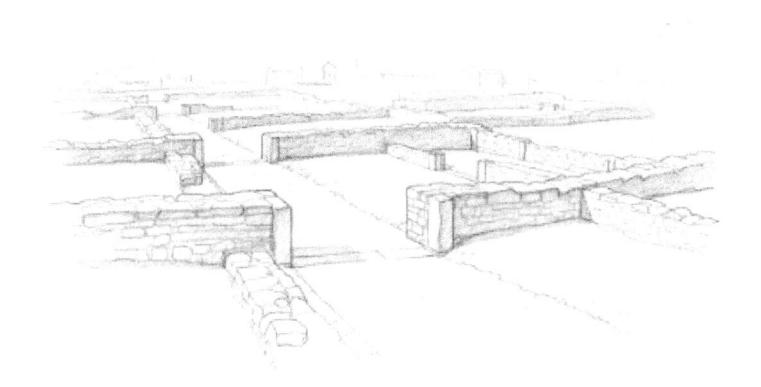

6. Saxon Period: From Burhs to Bjarn's Gate (410 AD - 1066 AD)

Following the Roman withdrawal, Newark transformed into a fortified Saxon burh, with its name likely derived from "Neue Werk" or "New Work," referencing a new defensive structure. A coin from King Edwy and over 300 urns from an Anglo-Saxon cremation cemetery at Millgate—bearing designs linked to Northern Germany and Denmark—suggest early Anglo-Saxon settlement. Viking influence is etched into street names like Kirk Gate and Barnby Gate, while Lady Godiva's 11th-century ownership marked Newark's transition into ecclesiastical hands, setting the stage for its medieval prominence.

7. Medieval Period: Castles, Kings, and Market Things
(1066 AD - 1485 AD)

Newark's medieval rise was anchored by the construction of Newark Castle in the 12th century by Bishop Alexander of Lincoln. Strategically located on the River Trent and the Fosse Way, the town became a military and commercial hub. King John died here in 1216, and the following year, William Marshal launched the Battle of Lincoln Fair from Newark. The town's market, granted Wednesday trading rights by King John in 1213, became a regional staple. By the 13th century, Newark's population exceeded 1,000, and its reputation as "The Key to the North" was firmly established.

8. Tudor Period: Wool, Wealth & Winking at the Crown
(1485 AD - 1603 AD)

The Tudor era saw Newark flourish through agriculture and the booming wool trade. Flemish weavers like Alan Fleming brought expertise that turned Newark into a textile powerhouse, with exports reaching Bruges and Ghent. Fullers, tanners, and shoemakers supported a thriving leather industry, while inns like The Old White Hart catered to travelers along the Great North Road. The 1487 Battle of Stoke Field, fought nearby, marked the end of the Wars of the Roses. Surviving Tudor buildings like the White Hart Hotel and Prince Rupert Pub still echo the town's prosperous past.

9. Stuart Period: Stuart Shenanigans (1603–1714)

The Stuart period thrust Newark into the heart of the English Civil War, where it became a Royalist stronghold due to its strategic location. Newark Castle and the town endured three sieges, with figures like King Charles I, Sir Richard Byron, and Lord Belasyse shaping its wartime story. Despite bombardments, disease, and starvation, Newark held firm until surrendering in 1646. Post-war, the town rebuilt and resumed its role as a market center. The Restoration brought stability, but the scars of war remained etched in Newark's landscape and collective memory.

10. Georgian Period: Grandeur, Growth & Genteel Gossip
(1714–1837)

In the Georgian era, Newark embraced elegance and Enlightenment ideals. Brick and stone replaced timber, and landmarks like the neoclassical Town Hall and Ossington Coffee Palace became civic and social hubs. The market thrived, malting and brewing industries expanded, and local banks financed growth. Education and scientific societies flourished, reflecting a town in intellectual bloom. With its refined architecture, economic vitality, and cultural sophistication, Georgian Newark was a model of progress and prosperity

11. The Victorian Era: Industrial Revolution: Steam, Steel, and Stubborn Progress (1837 - 1901)

The Industrial Revolution transformed Newark with the arrival of the Midland Railway in 1846, linking it to national trade routes. Factories and foundries, including the Ransome & Marles Bearing Company, powered the economy. Urban development brought terraced housing, improved sanitation, and public health reforms. Victorian architecture flourished, with restorations to St. Mary Magdalene Church and the Town Hall. Social life revolved around alehouses and education, with institutions like the Newark Ragged School offering new opportunities to the working class.

12. The 20th Century: Wars, Recovery, and Modern Marvels

Newark's 20th century was marked by resilience through two world wars. The town supported the war effort with munitions production and RAF operations, enduring tragedies like the 1941 bombing of Ransome & Marles. Post-war recovery brought housing, schools, and infrastructure, while the 1960s ushered in cultural change. The late century saw industrial diversification and digital adoption. Events like the Newark Show and Queen Elizabeth II's 1977 visit highlighted community spirit, while the Great Flood of 1947 tested and proved the town's solidarity.

13. 21st Century: Newark in the New Millennium: A Town with a Plan (and a Map)(2000–Present)

AIn the 21st century, Newark has embraced digital heritage and community pride. The Newark-on-Trent Photographs group and Newark Guide website have fostered local engagement, while the National Civil War Centre has made history accessible and interactive. Green spaces like Sconce and Devon Park offer natural retreats, and the rise of glamping has drawn new visitors. Photography and social media have become tools for storytelling, connecting residents through shared history and scenic beauty. Newark continues to evolve, blending its rich past with a forward-looking spirit.

Notable Historic Sites

MillGate

Info Provided by Millgate Conservation Society

The Millgate area – consternation and conservation

These days, a saunter around the Millgate Conservation Area, with its pretty river frontage and charming buildings, is a relaxed, Sunday afternoon sort of experience. But 'twasn't always so.

In 400AD, you might have been shoved out of the way by a cohort of marching soldiers - Millgate follows the route of Fosse Way, once one of England's busiest Roman roads.

In the mid-1600s you'd have found a population at war with itself.

In the 18th and 19th centuries, you'd have been attacked by the Industrial Revolution. The area, especially Millgate itself and the parallel Navigation canal, was a bedlam of manufacturing and commerce. Your senses would have been assaulted by the ugliness, cacophony and stench of grinding mills and factories, breweries and malting houses, fellmongers and a tannery. And people. Shops and street traders, draught horses and barges, pubs and preachers all contributed to the general uproar.

And in the 21st century you'll be confronted by their ghosts – if you know how and where to look.

Where Castlegate meets Millgate - known as Hill End - you'll find a row of buildings that once included a plumber's, a basket maker's and a butcher's premises. Two of them (60 and 62) have been immaculately restored as period cottages by a local, gentleman builder. Plunge down Top Lock Passage (mind the dog!) and you'll find yourself beside the Navigation canal, with its picturesque lock, lock keeper's cottages and unrivalled, panoramic views of Newark Castle and Trent Bridge. If it's sunny, the Swan & Salmon serves lunch and chilled light ale on its riverside balcony...

But if you do have to push on, cross over the lock, turn left, and you'll discover more photo opportunities. Mill Bridge has spectacular views. Parnham's Island - once the site of a water-powered flour mill - is now a haven for anglers. Further along, there's a multi-arched bridge over a weir, where the Navigation cascades into the Trent.

Or stay on the south bank, and follow the Riverside Walk, with its procession of yards and wharves, warehouses, mills and industrial buildings. The character of the original seed mill is still there - now housing a yoga studio - but nowadays you'll also find chic town houses, swish apartments, and no fewer than three architects' practices. Not to mention the Navigation pub with its industrial-era interior and waterside views. Mind your head, but also look at that floor.

More ghosts of Millgate past await on the main street. Dating back to the 1500s, numbers 1 and 3 are allegedly the oldest in the street. Nos 5-9 were probably built in the 1780s. What sort of people lived in them? In 1871, for example, the row was occupied by a laundress, a shoemaker, a wood turner, a provisions dealer and a coal yard labourer. Nowadays, there's a planning consultant, a retired craftsman, an ex-marketing executive and an art director. In living memory, No 9 was a pump shop and then a crêperie (presumably with the front door worked back then).

The small, but elegant houses opposite were designed in the 1980s, by architect David Pickles OBE – proving that it is possible, with enough sensibility, to create modern housing that blends seamlessly with the character of the area, whilst adding to its aesthetic appeal. Best of all, David still lives on the street he helped create.

Next door to these homes are fine Georgian residences, some with blanked out windows. Not the infamous Window Tax; merely Georgian architects following their obsession with uniformity and visual balance.

But talking of tax. There was once a Brick Tax; so the builders of No 33 included extra-long bricks to reduce the number required. Tax evasion or avoidance?

A wealthy milling family – the Bilsons – owned the Georgian pile at No 23, whilst 35 and 37 were once Victorian shops; their fronts still evident.

On the corner of Pelham Street stands the last ghost of Newark's famed malting industry; now a boxing club. Pause here, listen carefully and you'll hear the gurgling of St Catherine's well, gushing along beneath your feet. Walk on and you'll have quaint cottages on one hand and, on the other, the Millgate House Hotel – at one time a Waifs and Strays Society home for destitute girls.

And so the parade continues, with quiet passages leading to hidden yards, with names like Taylor's and Cottam's. Beside Navigation Yard, with its quaint houses, history lies underfoot; here are cobble ladders – originally designed to help overburdened draught horses find enough traction to overcome the gradient between Weighbridge Wharf and Millgate. These days Weighbridge Wharf is (weirdly) an otter park.

Tannery Wharf, meanwhile, is an imposing piece of period industrial chic, now residential. And amidst the historic names there's a waterfront feature renamed after its current owner, just a few years ago. See if you can find Healy's Wharf.

Back on the main street; No 55 is a timber-framed house dating back to the 1500s. But here's a mystery; dendrochronology testing has revealed…55's timbers conform to no known dating matrix! Squires Yard is a modern iteration of an earlier building, which saw life as a Salvation Army barracks, wool and flax halls, a rope walk and a garage. The old Methodist chapel is now offices, whilst the Watermill pub (first licensed in 1794 and still serving in 2021) stands four square, awaiting the next phase in its colourful history.

But for a contemporary glimpse of times gone by, take in the scene through the Georgian archway between 69 and 71. Here is a working yard reflecting all the character of a bygone age. Step through the arch to buy logs or smokeless from the yard's owner, and you'll probably be given a ton of knowledge about local history – and miniature horses – into the bargain. You may even find one of his small horses grazing on the field outside the Old Hall (a presbytery reputedly built on the site of a medieval hermitage). Or, indeed, on the grassy verges beside Millgate Field - an ever-diminishing wildlife area adjacent to the new Marina Quays development.

But before the marina are historic buildings; some grand, some modest. (Hoity toity has always rubbed shoulders with hoi polloi in Millgate.) Lenton Terrace, for example, is a stand of quality Victorian townhouses, flanking a ginnel that leads to no less than eight period cottages with vaulted cellars that were rented out to the adjacent Trent Brewery. Further along, the painter and Mayor W.H. Cubley lived at Nos 80-82.

The White House, meanwhile, is probably Millgate's most imposing pile – boasting 17th century origins, Georgian and Edwardian refinements and a history of illustrious residents; ranging from mill owners to a Liberal MP, a steel wire manufacturer and a wealthy local land owner.

You're now standing in what some locals - somewhat self-consciously - refer to as Lower Millgate. It's a hopeful attempt to distinguish it from the more rough-and-ready 'Town End' and, in truth, you will find some of the Millgate area's most appealing buildings here. Crow View, for example, is arguably one of the most desirable, and handsome, houses in Newark. Built around 1830, it stands on the corner of King Street – a site which marks the edge of the fortifications that defended Newark from the besieging Parliamentarians (1645-6) during the English Civil War. Just round the corner, in King Street itself, there's a neat contrast to the opulence of Crow View; the National School. This simple little building was founded in 1840 to provide education for around 200 poor children. In the 20th century it became the studio of prominent artist Robert Kiddey.

Returning to the theme of the English Civil War. Walk past the Georgian townhouses to your left on Millgate (they were built on the site of a Saxon cremation cemetery), cross the Farndon Road at the Spring House pub (the name was inspired by nearby St Catherine's Well) and you'll come to a delightful park. The Queen's Sconce is the site of the earthwork fort built to defend Newark, and command the strategically important river and Great North Road, during the conflict's sieges. The space was also used as bleaching field by Scales Linen Mill on Farndon Road, and as a prisoner of war camp during World War Two. Today the Sconce is both an historic monument and a park offering a playground, café and a leafy walk along the River Devon (pronounced Deevon locally, of course).

And so ends this insight into Millgate. But the final – and most fitting – summation of the area comes from the late Doctor David Marcombe, historian, author and former local resident;

"Pevsner commented on Millgate's 'villagey atmosphere' and it is still true to say that this fashionable area of Newark has a very firm character of its own. This rests not only on its distinctive architectural heritage, but also on the unusual range of people who live there, including students; manual workers; and professionals. But, surprisingly, this is as it always has been."

Article written by MCS, with special thanks to Ann Marcombe for her invaluable contribution. Reference: 'Millgate: a Guided Walk' by David and Ann Marcombe.

Ad Pontem – Newark's Roman Service Station

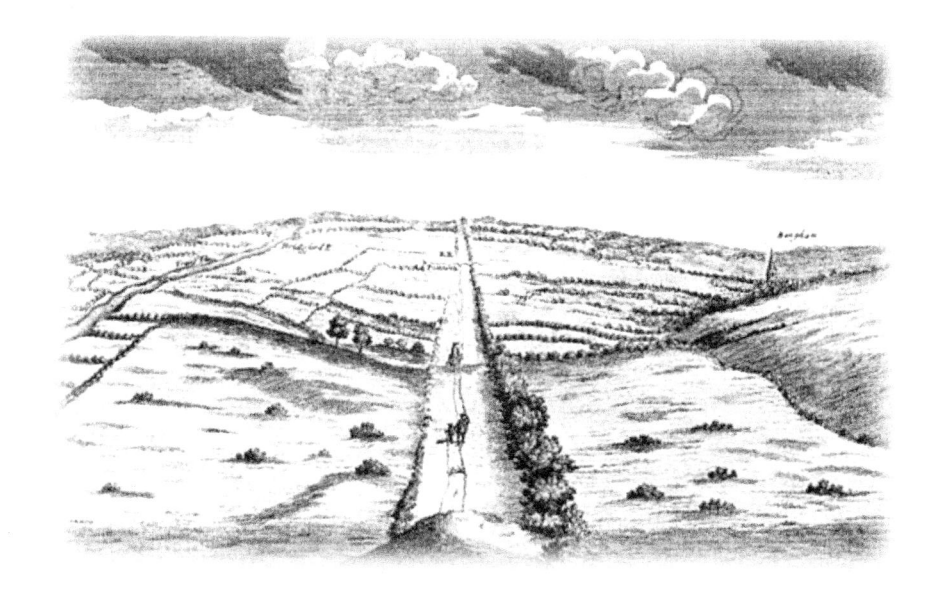

Long before Newark-on-Trent became known for its castle, Civil War sieges, and excellent tea rooms, it was a strategic pit stop for Roman soldiers, traders, and anyone brave enough to wear sandals year-round. Welcome to Ad Pontem, Latin for "by the bridge" — a name that's as practical as it is poetic.

A Bridge Too Useful

Ad Pontem was established near a crossing of the River Trent, along the Fosse Way, one of Roman Britain's major highways. If you were travelling from Exeter to Lincoln in the 1st century AD (and who wasn't?), this was your go-to layover. Think of it as the Roman equivalent of a motorway service station — only with more spears and fewer overpriced sandwiches.

Fortified Convenience

This wasn't just a roadside snack stop. Ad Pontem featured a fortlet — a small military encampment with ramparts and a double-ditch defensive system. Covering about 1¼ acres, it was designed to keep out troublemakers and keep in the legionnaires. Nearby, a larger polygonal enclosure spanned over 5 acres, with the Fosse Way cutting right through it. Roman efficiency at its finest.

Life at Ad Pontem

The settlement was more than just a military outpost. Archaeological digs have unearthed coins, pottery, glassware, iron tools, and even painted wall plaster — suggesting that some residents lived in style. It was occupied from the late 1st century to at least the 4th century, which means it outlasted most reality TV shows and a few Roman emperors.

Newark's Ancient Neighbour

Though Ad Pontem is technically closer to the village of Brough, its legacy is woven into the fabric of Newark-on-Trent. Artifacts from the site are housed in museums across the region, including Newark itself. So if you're in town and fancy a bit of time travel, pop into the local museum and marvel at the relics of Newark's Roman past.

What's Left Today?

Not much is visible on the surface — unless you're an archaeologist with a drone and a dream. But the site is protected as a Scheduled Monument, and its story continues to intrigue historians and locals alike. It's a reminder that Newark's history didn't start with castles and cannonballs — it started with sandals and stone roads.

Crococalana – The Roman Town That Time (Almost) Forgot

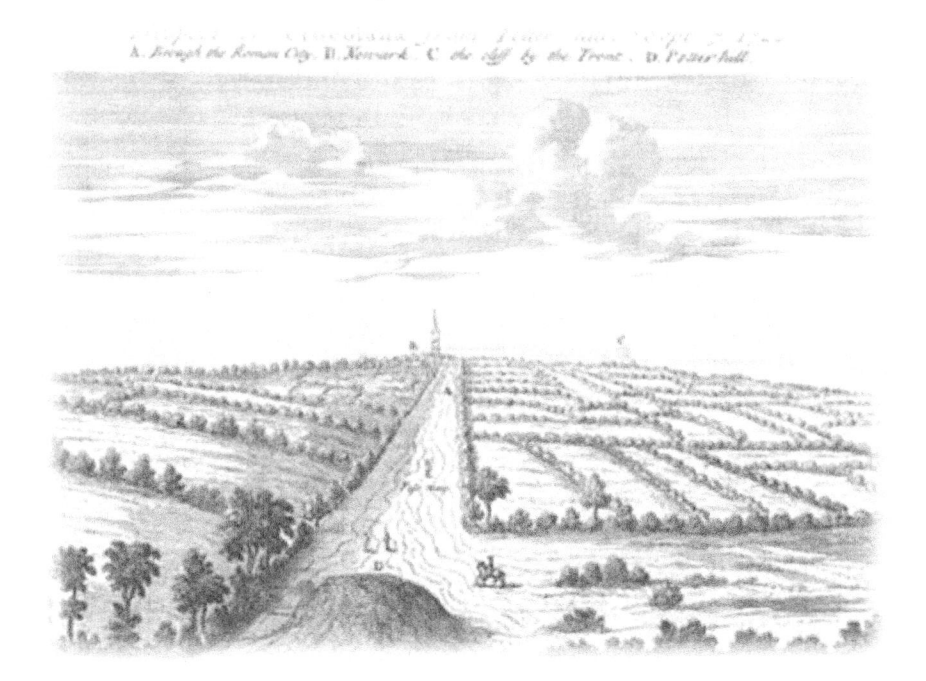

If you've ever driven through the Nottinghamshire countryside and thought, "This field looks suspiciously historic," you might have been passing over the remains of Crococalana — a Roman town with a name that sounds like a prehistoric creature but was, in fact, a thriving settlement just a few miles from modern-day Newark-on-Trent.

What's in a Name?
Crococalana (try saying that three times fast) was a Roman town located near the present-day village of Brough, just northeast of Newark. Its name appears in the Antonine Itinerary, a sort of Roman satnav from the 2nd century AD. While scholars still debate the exact meaning, it's safe to say it was more about roads and rest stops than reptiles.

Location, Location, Legion
Strategically plonked along the Fosse Way, Crococalana was the Roman equivalent of a motorway junction — minus the Greggs. It sat between Margidunum (near Bingham) and Lindum Colonia (modern Lincoln), making it a key stop for soldiers, merchants, and anyone else brave enough to travel in sandals.

The site was a rectangular defended area, roughly 700 by 500 feet, surrounded by ditches. Inside, archaeologists have found crop marks indicating pits, floors, and walls — basically, the Roman version of a housing estate. There's even evidence of a separate enclosure with a rectangular building, possibly a mansio (a kind of Roman Travelodge for officials).

Digging Up the Past

Excavations have unearthed coins, pottery, glassware, iron tools, and objects made of bronze, bone, and horn. The presence of painted wall plaster suggests that some of the buildings were quite posh—think underfloor heating and mosaic envy. Crococalana wasn't just a military outpost; it was a proper town with infrastructure, trade, and probably a few gossiping neighbours.

Newark's Roman Roots

While Crococalana itself lies just outside Newark's modern boundaries, its influence was felt throughout the region. The Fosse Way connected it directly to Ad Pontem and Margidunum, forming a Roman triangle of trade, travel, and tactical advantage. Newark-on-Trent, though not a Roman town itself, owes much of its early development to the infrastructure laid down by these ancient neighbours.

What's There Now?

Today, Crococalana is mostly farmland. No grand ruins, no columns, no toga-clad tour guides. But beneath the soil lies a rich archaeological record, and the site is protected as a Scheduled Monument. Artifacts from Crococalana can be found in museums across the East Midlands, including Newark's own National Civil War Centre—because why not mix your Romans with your Roundheads?

Conclusion: A Town Worth Remembering

Crococalana may not have the fame of Pompeii or the glamour of Rome, but it played a vital role in the Romanisation of Britain—and in the early story of Newark-on-Trent. So next time you're driving past Brough, give a little wave to the fields. You're passing through history, even if it's wearing a very convincing disguise of wheat.

Margidunum – The Roman Roundabout Before Newark

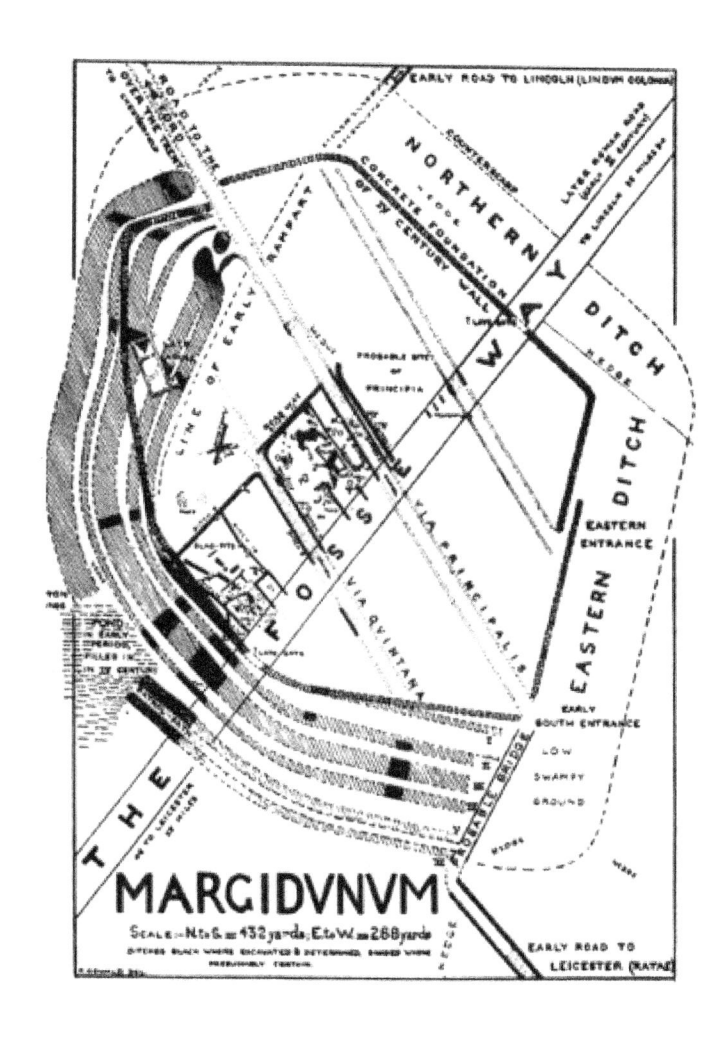

Before Newark-on-Trent became a hotspot for castles, cannonballs, and cream teas, it was surrounded by Roman settlements that made the area a logistical dream for toga-clad travellers. One such place was Margidunum, a name that sounds like a spell from Harry Potter but was actually a bustling Roman town just up the Fosse Way from Newark.

Welcome to the Roman Services

Margidunum, meaning something like "fort by the edge" (or possibly "place where sandals go to die"), was located near modern-day Bingham, just a short chariot ride from Newark. It sat proudly on the Fosse Way, the Roman Empire's answer to the M1, connecting Exeter to Lincoln. If Ad Pontem was the service station with a scenic view, Margidunum was the full-on Roman rest stop—complete with shops, barracks, and probably a few grumpy centurions.

A Fortified Frontier

Established in the 1st century AD, Margidunum began life as a military fort, keeping an eye on the locals and the road. But as the years rolled on and the empire settled in, it evolved into a civilian town. Think less "marching orders" and more "market stalls." Archaeologists have uncovered evidence of roads, buildings, and even a bathhouse—because even Roman soldiers needed a good soak after a long day of empire-building.

What's in a Name?
Margidunum was one of the key waypoints between Ad Pontem and Lindum Colonia (modern-day Lincoln). It was Newark's older, slightly more organised cousin—less drama, more drainage. Its strategic location made it a vital cog in the Roman machine, helping to move troops, goods, and gossip across Britannia.

Digging Up the Past
Excavations at Margidunum have revealed pottery, coins, and the remains of buildings that suggest a community. There's even evidence of a Roman temple, which means the locals weren't just trading—they were praying too. Possibly for better weather or fewer taxes.

Newark's Roman Neighbourhood
While Margidunum itself isn't within Newark's modern boundaries, its influence certainly was. The road that connected it to Ad Pontem ran right through what would become Newark-on-Trent. So, in a way, Newark owes its very existence to the Romans' obsession with straight roads and orderly towns.

Today's Margidunum
Today, there's not much left to see on the surface—unless you're an archaeologist or a very optimistic metal detectorist. But the site is protected, and its story lives on in museums and local lore. If you're ever driving the A46 near Bingham, give a little nod to the fields—you're passing through history.

Queen Sconce

Queen's Sconce in Newark-on-Trent is a significant historical fortification with a rich past. Here's a detailed look at its history

Early History

Queen's Sconce was constructed in 1644 during the First English Civil War to protect the Royalist garrison based at Newark Castle. The fortification was named after Queen Henrietta Maria, the wife of King Charles I. Newark was a key strategic location due to its position at the crossing of the River Trent and the intersection of the Great North Road and Fosse Way.

Architectural Features

The sconce is an earthwork fortification, designed in a star shape when viewed from above. It measures approximately 120 meters by 133 meters, with a height of up to 9 meters. The structure includes angle bastions projecting from the south, southwest, north, and northeast, which were possible platforms for artillery. The ramparts and bastions are enclosed by a ditch up to 21 meters wide and 4.5 meters deep.

Historical Significance

Queen's Sconce played a crucial role during the sieges of Newark. The town was besieged three times by Parliamentary forces before it finally surrendered in May 1646. The fortification was part of a network of defences that helped the Royalists maintain control over Newark for much of the war. The sconce is one of the few surviving examples of Civil War earthworks in the country

Modern Era

Today, Queen's Sconce is part of Sconce and Devon Park, Newark's largest open space. The park includes a visitor centre, nature reserve, and various recreational facilities. The sconce itself is a listed ancient monument, recognized for its historical and architectural significance. Visitors can explore the fortification and learn about its role in the Civil War through interpretive displays and guided tours.

The Battle OF Lincoln Fair: The Battle That Saved England (and Newarks role in it)

Picture it: England, 1217. The Magna Carta (June 15, 1215) is barely dry, King Johns corpse was only removed from Newark castle 7 months ago (19 October 1216) - good riddance, some say, and his nine-year-old son, Henry III, is now king.

But not everyone is cheering. A group of rebellious barons has invited Prince Louis of France (Le Lion) to take the English crown. He's already in London, sipping mead and swagging around like he owns the place. (In 1216, during the First Barons' War over the English succession, Prince Louis of France entered London and proclaimed himself King of England. Louis was supported by various English barons who resisted the rule of King John)

Back to 1217, in the loyalist stronghold of Newark-on-Trent, the mood is tense but determined. This market town, known for its strategic location and excellent pies (probably), is about to become the launchpad for a counterstrike that will change the course of English history.

Enter The legendary knight William Marshal , Earl of Pembroke and regent to young Henry. At the ripe age of 70, he's still got more fight in him than a tavern full of Saxons on payday. Marshal called all nobles holding castles in England to a muster in Newark......And what a turnout!

From Newark's cobbled streets and timber-framed inns emerged:
- 400 knights (shiny armour, sharp swords, and probably a few egos)
- 250 crossbowmen (the medieval equivalent of snipers)
- A motley crew of mounted and foot soldiers ready to march on Lincoln

Marshal's army sets off from Newark with purpose — and probably a few blisters, towards Lincoln.

The city had fallen to Louis, but Lincoln Castle, perched defiantly on its hill, was still held by the indomitable Nicola de la Haie, a castellan loyal to Henry III. She had been holding out against the siege.

On 20 May 1217, Marshal's forces arrive at Lincoln and launch a surprise attack through the West Gate. The French and rebel barons are caught off guard. The fighting is fierce, but the loyalists have the upper hand. Thomas, Count of Perche, leading the French forces, refuses to surrender and is killed in the melee.

The French lines collapse. The rebels flee. The siege is lifted. And just like that, the tide of the war turns (The battle lasted around 6 hours)

Now, about that name. The aftermath of the battle saw the victorious troops sack the city of Lincoln. The looting was so extensive and, frankly, so enthusiastic, that it became known as the "Lincoln Fair" — a darkly humorous jab at the idea of a medieval market. Instead of buying goods, the soldiers helped themselves.

It was brutal, but effective. The message was clear: back the wrong side, and you'll pay in silver and soot.

From Newark's perspective, this was a moment of triumph. The town wasn't just a waypoint — it was the strategic nerve centre of the loyalist campaign. It was here that Marshal's army assembled, planned, and prayed. Without Newark, there might not have been a victory at Lincoln. And without Lincoln, there might not have been an England as we know it.

227

The Battle of Lincoln was the turning point in the First Barons' War. Many of Henry's enemies – barons who had supported Louis, and who helped supply, organise and command Louis's military forces – were captured at Lincoln. French reinforcements, under the command of Eustace the Monk, were then sent across the English Channel to bolster Louis's forces. The French ships were defeated by Hubert de Burgh in the Battle of Dover. This defeat greatly reduced the French threat to the English crown and Prince Louis and his remaining forces returned to France. In September 1217, the Treaty of Lambeth forced Louis to give up his claim to the English throne and to eject Eustace's brothers from the Channel Islands.

And Newark? It returned to its peaceful rhythms, its market stalls, and its quiet pride in having played a part in one of the most pivotal moments in medieval history.

The Battle of Stoke Field

The Battle of Stoke Field, fought on June 16, 1487, near East Stoke in Nottinghamshire, is considered the last significant battle of the Wars of the Roses. Here's a detailed look at its history

The Wars of the Roses were caused by the protracted struggle for power between the dynasties of the House of Lancaster (red rose) and the competing House of York (white rose).

The battle was the last major conflict between the Houses of York and Lancaster and was a battle to gain control of the crown. The Battle of Bosworth Field, two years previously, had established King Henry VII on the throne, ending the last period of Yorkist rule and initiating that of the Tudors.

Background

The battle was a decisive engagement between the forces of Henry VII, the first Tudor king, and the Yorkist supporters of Lambert Simnel, a pretender to the throne. Despite Henry VII's victory at the Battle of Bosworth in 1485, which ended Richard III's reign and established the Tudor dynasty, Yorkist opposition persisted.

The Battle of Stoke Field was an attempt to unseat King Henry VII in favour of a 10 year old boy called Lambert Simnel who was an imposter pretending to be Edward, Earl of Warwick, the son of Edward IV's brother, the Duke of Clarence. Simnel was used as a pawn by leading Yorkists to try and re-establish their hold on the crown

Key Figures
Henry VII: The reigning king, leading the Lancastrian forces.
John de la Pole, Earl of Lincoln: A leading Yorkist claimant who supported Lambert Simnel.
Lambert Simnel: A young boy presented as Edward, Earl of Warwick, a Yorkist heir.

The Battle
The Yorkist forces, numbering around 8,000, included German and Swiss mercenaries provided by Margaret of Burgundy. They took up a defensive position on Rampire Hill

Henry VII's army, led by the Earl of Oxford, was slightly larger, with about 15,000 men.

The hill they formed up on is known as Burrand Furlong and a stone put there by Newark Archaeological and Local History Society (NALHS) in 1987 marks the spot where Henry VII supposedly planted his standard after the battle. We believe Henry VII's army to have been around 15,000, with John de Vere, Earl of Oxford leading the vanguard of around 6,000 who approached along the Upper Fossse, which crossed what is now Syerston Airfield and continues along Humber Lane and down into the village.

The main battle, led by Henry VII, probably consisted of around 6,000 with the rearguard, led by Lord Strange. It might be worth mentioning the Irish Kerns, who were poorly armed and armoured. One account speaks about them being shot through with arrows 'like hedgehogs' and it was probably there annihilation by the archers that led to the rout. Other key persons involved were Martin Schwartz, leader of the mercenary Landsknechts and Thomas Fitzgerald, leader of the Irish, both of whom were killed.

Outcome
The battle ended in a decisive victory for Henry VII. The Yorkist forces were routed, with many killed in the fighting or pursued and cut down as they fled. Key Yorkist leaders, including the Earl of Lincoln, were killed, effectively ending organized Yorkist resistance.

The Battlefield witnessed the death of up to 7,000 soldiers and the river is said to have ran red with their blood

The Red Gutter is said to be the area where the massacre took place, although it is unclear whether this natural escarpment is so called due the blood split there during the battle or whether it derives its name from red clay deposits.

Historical Significance
The Battle of Stoke Field is often considered the last battle of the Wars of the Roses. It solidified Henry VII's hold on the throne and marked the end of major Yorkist attempts to reclaim it. The victory also helped to secure the Tudor dynasty's future, allowing Henry VII to focus on consolidating his rule and stabilizing the kingdom

The Newark Torc – Newark's Golden Halo of Mystery

Long before Newark-on-Trent became known for its market stalls, Civil War sieges, and suspiciously enthusiastic reenactors, it was already making headlines — albeit 2,000 years too early for the Newark Advertiser. Enter the Newark Torc: a dazzling Iron Age neck ornament that proves even ancient Britons knew how to accessorise with flair.

Discovery: From Tree Surgeon to Treasure Hunter

In February 2005, Maurice Richardson, a local tree surgeon with a metal detector and a hunch, stumbled upon what would become one of the most significant finds of Iron Age Celtic gold jewellery in half a century. While most of us find bottle caps and rusty nails in fields, Maurice found a 700-gramme gold alloy torc — because Newark doesn't do things by halves

The torc was buried in a pit on the outskirts of town, not lost in a drunken Iron Age stumble as one might hope, but deliberately hoarded. Possibly as an offering to the gods. Or perhaps just hidden by someone who didn't trust Iron Age banks. Either way, it was declared a **national treasure** (just with less Nicholas Cage) and acquired for Newark's Museum (now part of the National Civil War Centre) in 2006, thanks to a hefty grant from the National Heritage Memorial Fund

Design: Gold, Glamour, and a Bit of Norfolk

The Newark Torc is made from a mix of gold, silver, and copper — because plain gold is just too basic. It measures 20 cm in diameter and weighs in at a neck-straining 1.5 pounds. The body is formed from eight finely plaited wires twisted into a single rope, ending in ring-shaped terminals adorned with floral and point-work designs. It's the Iron Age equivalent of haute couture.

Experts believe it was made or finished by the same person as another torc found in Netherurd in Scotland.. This suggests either a travelling goldsmith with a flair for symmetry or a very niche Iron Age Etsy shop.

There is also suggestion that the Torc was stolen by Vikings at one point!!

Purpose: Jewellery, Power Symbol, or Ritual Bling?

What was the torc for? No one knows for sure. It could have been a status symbol, a religious offering, or simply the Iron Age version of a flex. Jeremy Hill of the British Museum described it as "an extraordinary object" showing "an incredibly high level of technological skill and artistry"

In other words, it wasn't your average neckwear.

Theories abound: perhaps it was worn by a tribal leader, a druid, or someone who just really wanted to be noticed at the local roundhouse gathering. Whatever the case, it was buried with care, suggesting reverence — or at least a very cautious owner.

Legacy: Newark's Shining Star

Today, the Newark Torc is proudly displayed at the National Civil War Centre, where it gleams under glass and sits there, judging your jewellery choices and demanding you add more bling to your life. It's been featured on the BBC, in academic journals, and in the dreams of every amateur detectorist in the East Midlands.

It stands as a testament to Newark's long and glittering history — proof that even in 200 BC, the people of this town had a taste for the finer things. And while we may never know exactly who wore it or why, one thing's certain: Newark-on-Trent has always had a golden touch.

For more info on torcs, check out the fantastic Tess Machlings big book of Torcs - https://bigbookoftorcs.com/

Twelve Sides of Confusion – The Norton Disney Dodecahedron

In the pantheon of archaeological oddities, few objects have inspired as much scholarly head-scratching and speculative mumbling as the Roman dodecahedron. And in 2023, Newark-on-Trent found itself unexpectedly thrust into this ancient enigma when the Norton Disney History and Archaeology Group unearthed one in a field just outside town. Because of course they did.

Discovery: Unearthed by Enthusiasts, Not Aliens

It was June 2023, and while most of the country was busy arguing about potholes and bin days, a group of local archaeologists were digging up history — literally. What they found was a 12-sided copper alloy object, roughly the size of a satsuma, and about as easy to explain. It was the first of its kind discovered in the Midlands and one of only 33 known in Britain. That's rarer than a functioning fax machine.

The object was found in situ (in the original place), nestled beside 4th-century Roman pottery in what appeared to be a quarry pit. It was in excellent condition, which is more than can be said for most of us after a day in the Nottinghamshire sun.

Description: A Dodecahedron by Any Other Name

The Norton Disney Dodecahedron is made of 75% copper, 7% tin, and 18% lead — basically the Roman version of a mystery meat pie. Each of its twelve pentagonal faces has a circular hole in the centre, and the whole thing is cast with a level of precision that suggests either ritual significance or a very bored metallurgist.

It's not standardised in size, shows no signs of wear, and doesn't appear in any Roman texts. Which means it's either a sacred object, a child's toy, or the ancient equivalent of a paperweight that no one wanted to admit they didn't understand.

Theories: Ritual, Religion, or Really No Idea

Scholars have proposed everything from candlestick holders to astronomical devices to knitting gauges. But the most plausible theory is that these dodecahedra were used in religious or ritual contexts — possibly linked to the mounted horseman deity discovered nearby in 1989. Because nothing says "divine power" like a twelve-holed polygon.

Of course, it could also have been a very elaborate way to lose your marbles.

Legacy: Newark's Most Mathematical Mystery

Today, the Norton Disney Dodecahedron is proudly displayed at the National Civil War Centre in Newark, where it silently judges visitors who can't remember their GCSE geometry (te smug little scamper). It's also been featured on the BBC's *Digging for Britain*, which is the archaeological equivalent of being knighted.

The Myth of the Newark Tunnels

Newark-on-Trent is a town rich in history, with tales of kings, battles, and ancient architecture. But among its many stories, one persistent myth has captured the imagination of locals and visitors alike: the legend of the Newark Tunnels.

A Town Beneath the Town?

For generations, rumors have swirled about a network of tunnels running beneath Newark. These subterranean passages are said to connect various historic sites, from the castle to the church, and even to the Friary. The idea of secret tunnels used for clandestine activities, hidden escapes, or smuggling has a certain romantic allure. But is there any truth to these tales?

The Wing Tavern and Other Legends

One of the most famous tunnel tales involves the Wing Tavern pub, which reportedly had a door in the cellar floor leading to a mysterious passage. However, personal accounts suggest that this "tunnel" was merely a short length of cellar heading towards the church. Similarly, rumors of a tunnel between the Friary, Newark Castle, and the church have never been substantiated.

The Search for Evidence

Over the years, various investigations have sought to uncover the truth behind the tunnel myth. In 2013, an archaeological study using ground-penetrating radar found no evidence of tunnels under the Market Place, though it did reveal extended cellars and medieval walls.
A 2014 documentary explored the cellars beneath shops around the town, but failed to establish any concrete connections.

In 2018, a more extensive radar survey funded by lottery money aimed to settle the question once and for all. The results were disappointing for tunnel enthusiasts: no tunnels were found, only extensive cellars. Kevin Winter of the Newark Town Centre Hidden Heritage Group noted that while the findings were not definitive, they strongly suggested that the tunnels were a myth.

Why the Myth Persists

Despite the lack of evidence, the tunnel myth endures. Perhaps it's the allure of hidden history, or the thrill of imagining secret passages beneath our feet. Or maybe it's just the fun of a good story. As James Wright, a building archaeologist, points out, tales of underground passages are common in many towns and villages. They often connect contrasting locations, like a manor house and a nunnery, adding a hint of scandal to the mix.

The Practicalities of Tunnel Building

The geology of Newark makes the construction of extensive tunnels unlikely. Unlike Nottingham, which is riddled with tunnels due to its sandstone base, Newark's clay-based soil and proximity to the river would have made tunnel construction difficult. The tunnels would have been hard to keep secret, expensive to build, and challenging to maintain.

The Final Verdict

While the idea of tunnels beneath Newark is tantalizing, the evidence suggests that they are more myth than reality. The interconnected cellars, extended for practical purposes like storage during the coaching era, likely gave rise to the tunnel tales. As Mr. Winter aptly put it, "People have loved to believe there were tunnels under Newark."

So, the next time you hear a story about the Newark Tunnels, enjoy it for what it is: a charming piece of local folklore that adds a touch of mystery to this historic town.

Fun Fact

The Wing Tavern pub was opened in protest by a landlord who was forced to close the Green Dragon pub to allow the final wing of the town hall to be built. The last remaining part of this pub is now known as Newark's thinnest house.

The Old Walls and Gates of Newark-on-Trent

Newark-on-Trent once boasted impressive walls and gates that encircled its medieval heart. While no physical remains of these ancient fortifications exist today, their legacy lives on through historical records, archaeological findings, and local lore.

The Elusive Walls

The old walls of Newark are a bit of a mystery. None of the existing plans show them, and the oldest maps only depict the town's defenses during the sieges, which were outside the line of the main walls. However, we can piece together their estimated locations based on historical accounts and the positions of the town's gates.

Mapping the Walls

Using various accounts, we can estimate the location of the walls. The walls possibly started at Trent Bridge, following the present line of Brewery Lane, Slaughterhouse Lane, and the Mount to Appleton Gate. From there, the wall turned south, running across Chauntry Park, behind the old Grammar School, and slightly east of Barnby Gate House. It then crossed Balderton Gate, turned southwest to Carter Gate, and continued down the north side of what is now Lombard Street (formerly Potterdyke) before crossing Castle Gate and reaching the river.

The Gates of Newark

Newark had three main gates: North Gate, East Gate, and South Gate. These gates were crucial for controlling access to the town and were often the focal points of defense during times of conflict.

North Gate (North Bar Gate)

Located near the current corner of Northgate and Slaughterhouse Lane, the North Gate was a stone wall with an arch, demolished in 1762. It was described as having a tall, narrow arch formed of thin slabs, with a double course of radially set voussoirs. This gate was a key entry point to the town from the north.

East Gate (Dry Bridge)

The East Gate, also known as Dry Bridge, stood in the middle of Bridge Street, near where Birds Bakery is today. It was taken down in 1784. Dr. Stukeley described it as a fine old arched gate of Roman work, with arches that were discovered during rebuilding efforts. The gate's position is now represented by buildings on either side of Bridge Street.

South Gate

The South Gate's position is defined in local deeds, indicating it was located at the end of Milnegate, near the corner of Pottergate. This gate controlled access to the town from the south and was an important part of Newark's defenses.

Archaeological Findings

Despite the lack of visible remains, archaeological studies have provided some insights into Newark's old walls. In 2013, a ground-penetrating radar survey found no evidence of tunnels under the Market Place but did locate extended cellars and earlier walls, likely dating back to medieval times. Further surveys in 2018 supported the idea that the town's defenses were primarily earthen ramparts rather than stone walls.

St Catherines Well

The Sacred Leprosy Healing Spring and The Legend of the Fair Maid of Newark

Long before Newark had polling stations or oversized houses, there was a holy well nestled near what is now Sconce and Devon Park. This wasn't just any spring — this was St Catherine's Well, a site so revered that it was believed to heal leprosy. Yes, leprosy. In an age when medicine involved more prayer than penicillin, this was a big deal .. ive added in the Legend at the bottom of this article (adds a splash of medieval romance)

To honour the miraculous waters, a chapel dedicated to St Catherine was built over the well. Pilgrims came, prayers were said, and the water flowed. But as centuries passed, the chapel disappeared — not with a bang, but with a quiet fade into history. Today, the well survives as a moss-covered, concrete-lined pond, tucked discreetly into a private ornamental garden.

Fast forward in time and the well found itself in the garden of St Catherine's Cottage, a charming white house that once served as a small convent. According to locals, you could still see the marks of the nuns' beds in the attic

The spring water, still flowing, was used to supply the house — purified, of course, because even holy water needs a filter these days

But then came the twist: the cottage was demolished in the 1980s to make way for a "HUGE house", as one local put it — a modern mansion that now guards the well like a dragon over treasure

A 2001 geophysical survey conducted at the site of St Catherine's Cottage revealed linear anomalies, possibly indicating the remains of back-filled ditches or other subsurface features

These findings suggest that the area may have had earlier structures or boundaries, possibly linked to the original chapel or convent that once stood near the well.

You can spot the brick culvert where the spring flows into the River Devon, about 100 yards upstream from the Devon Bridge

The Legend of the Fair Maid of Newark (14th Century)

According to Frank Earp's retelling, the well is tied to the tragic tale of Lady Isabel de Cauldwell, known as the Fair Maid of Newark.

Lady Isabel de Cauldwell was the daughter of a noble house, known not only for her beauty but for her kindness and grace.

Lady Isabel was admired by many, but two knights in particular vied for her affection: Sir Guy Saucimer and Sir Everard Bevercotes, Lord of Balderton. Childhood friends turned rivals, both men were brave, honourable, and deeply in love with Isabel. She, however, could not choose between them — her heart torn equally.

Frustrated, the knights gave her an ultimatum: choose one, and the other would accept her decision. But Isabel, unable to decide, left the matter to fate. The knights agreed to settle the matter by combat, trusting that God would favour the worthy.

On the eve of St Catherine's Day (23/24 Nov), the two knights met in a field by the River Devon. Lances shattered, swords clashed, and the duel raged into the night. Eventually, Sir Guy struck a fatal blow to Sir Everard, who fell to the ground, blood pouring from his wound. At that very spot, the earth opened and a spring of clear water burst forth — mingling with Everard's blood as it flowed to the river.

Sir Guy, horrified by what he had done, fled the scene.

When news reached the castle, Lady Isabel collapsed in grief. She died within hours, her heart broken. Meanwhile, Sir Guy, tormented by guilt, joined a band of pilgrims to Rome. Along the way, he was abandoned in France, stricken with leprosy — a punishment, he believed, for his sin.

He wandered the countryside in misery until one night, in a fevered dream, St Catherine appeared to him in radiant light. She told him that only the waters of the spring where he had slain his friend could heal him.

Sir Guy returned to England, confessed his sins, and was consecrated as a hermit. He made his way back to Newark and bathed in the spring. Miraculously, his leprosy was cured. In gratitude, he built a stone wall around the spring and a small chapel nearby, dedicating it to St Catherine. He lived out his days in piety, ministering to the sick and needy, and became known as St Guthred.

The spring, now known as St Catherine's Well, became a place of healing and pilgrimage. Though now hidden in a private garden near Sconce and Devon Park, its waters still flow.

The legend, first written down in the 15th century and later popularised by W. Dickinson in 1816, may blend folklore with fiction — but its emotional truth endures.

Even if the tale was embellished or invented, it draws on deep traditions of medieval storytelling: the love triangle, the duel of honour, the miraculous spring, and the redemptive power of faith.

Some say that on quiet evenings, when the wind rustles through the trees and the river runs slow, you can still feel her presence. A soft chill in the air. A ripple in the water. A whisper of silk and sorrow.

The well, now hidden in the grounds of a private home, may no longer be accessible to the public — but its legend lives on. In the name of the street nearby (Caldwell Drive, St Catherines Close, Saucemere Drive). In the memories of schoolchildren who once visited it. And in the hearts of those who still believe that love, honour, and sacrifice can leave a mark on the land.

1600's Disasters

The Great Flood of 1683: When Newark Got Absolutely Soaked (and Smashed)

If you think British winters are bad now, spare a thought for the residents of Newark-on-Trent in early 1683. After months of bone-chilling cold, the River Trent decided it had had enough of being frozen and staged a dramatic comeback—by flooding half the county.

This wasn't your average puddle. This was the Great Flood of 1683, a watery wallop that swept away bridges, drowned fields, and left Newark soggier than a Tudor sponge cake.

The trouble began with a brutal winter. From September 1682 to February 1683, Nottinghamshire endured a deep freeze so severe that the River Trent iced over completely

Locals reportedly skated on it, which sounds charming until you realise it was the prelude to disaster.

When the thaw finally came in early February, it wasn't gentle. It was a full-blown meltdown—literally. The sudden rise in temperature caused ice floes to break loose and surge downstream, turning the Trent into a medieval battering ram

The Town Bridge at Newark-on-Trent, a vital crossing point, was no match for the icy onslaught. The floodwaters and ice chunks swept away the bridge, leaving the town cut off and its riverside fields submerged

It was rebuilt by 1700, this time with a wooden deck on surviving stone piers

Meanwhile, nearby villages like Holme and North Muskham also bore the brunt of the flood, with damage reported across the Trent Valley. It was a regional disaster, but one that Newark weathered with its usual grit (and probably a lot of soggy shoes).

The Great Flood of 1683 didn't just wash away bridges—it reshaped Newark's relationship with the River Trent. It prompted stronger infrastructure, better planning, and a healthy respect for the river's unpredictable moods.

Today, Newark's bridges are sturdier, its flood defences (somewhat) smarter, and its residents (mostly) dry.

The Great Flood of 1683 was Newark-on-Trent's watery wake-up call. It was dramatic, destructive, and—let's be honest—probably quite cold. But it also showcased the town's resilience, its ability to rebuild, and its knack for turning even the worst disasters into stories worth telling.

So next time you cross the Trent, give a little nod to the river. And maybe check the weather forecast—just in case.

Newark and the Plague of 1645 – Newark-on-Trent's darkest hour

In the mid-17th century, Newark-on-Trent was not just a Royalist stronghold—it was also a town under siege from something far more insidious than cannonballs: plague and pestilence. The year 1645 marked the darkest chapter in Newark's Civil War saga, when disease swept through the town like an unwelcome guest who refused to leave.

Newark's strategic importance during the English Civil War made it a prime target for Parliamentarian forces. The town endured three sieges, with the final one in 1646 ending only when King Charles I ordered its surrender.

But before the cannons fell silent, the town was already groaning under the weight of disease According to historian Stuart B. Jennings, Newark in 1645 was described as "a miserable, stinking, infected town" -

The plague that year claimed an estimated 300 lives, roughly 15% of the population—a staggering toll for a town of around 2,000 souls Between 1642 and 1646, Newark recorded 835 burials, with a surplus of 196 burials over baptisms—a grim indicator of the town's suffering.

Typhus, known as "camp fever," was also rampant, especially during the winter months when cramped conditions and poor sanitation turned Newark into a petri dish of despair The plague's impact wasn't limited to Newark alone. Nearby villages like Balderton also suffered. In 1646, 129 people were buried in Balderton's churchyard due to the plague, coinciding with the final siege of Newark The convergence of warfare, overcrowding, and poor hygiene created the perfect storm for disease.

Soldiers, civilians, and livestock were packed into the town's narrow streets and makeshift shelters. As Lady Fanshawe observed during the siege of Oxford, "sometimes plague, sometimes sicknesses of other kinds, by reason of so many people packed together" Newark's role as a Royalist garrison meant it was constantly receiving reinforcements, supplies, and refugees—all potential carriers of disease.

The town's resilience was remarkable, but the cost was high. Today, the story of Newark's plague years is preserved in places like the National Civil War Centre, which documents the town's wartime and medical history The phrase "a miserable, stinking, infected town" may sound harsh, but it captures the brutal reality of life in Newark during the plague. Yet, amidst the death and despair, the town endured. Its people rebuilt, its markets reopened, and its history marched on.

Whispers from the other side: Unearthing Newark-on-Trent's Chilling Ghostly Encounters

Newark-on-Trent, a town steeped in centuries of dramatic history, doesn't just boast picturesque ruins and charming market squares. Oh no. Beneath its historic facade lies a spectral underbelly, a thriving community of the dearly departed who apparently missed the memo about moving on. If you're looking for a town that truly embraces its past, even the bit that goes bump in the night, then pull up a pew and prepare for some chilling tales.

I have to state here that I'm personally a firm skeptic when it comes to ghosts. My mind leans on facts, not spectral figures. Yet, the lore of a place, its chilling legends, the tales spread amongst a community and the sheer power of a good story utterly fascinate me. So, while I don't believe in literal hauntings, I'm captivated by how these tales weave into a town's history and character.

Let's kick things off with the grand dame herself, Newark Castle. This isn't just any old pile of stones; it's seen King John kick the bucket and endured the brutal English Civil War. So, naturally, it's a hotspot for spectral shenanigans.

Our starring role goes to the Hanging Ranger. Picture this: early 1900s, a castle ranger, a supposed illicit affair, and a tragic end in what was then the King's Bedroom. Visitors and guides alike claim to have witnessed his ghostly form, still twitching and jolting from the ceiling. Talk about a commitment to your craft, even in the afterlife!

But wait, there's more! The dungeons echo with hushed voices and chanting, while the oubliette (the "forgetting place" where prisoners were left to starve – cheerful, right?) leaves visitors with an overwhelming sense of dread. And if you hear screaming from the curtain wall by the river? That'll just be the faint echoes of Civil War anguish. Nothing to worry about. Probably.

Every good theatre has a resident ghost, and Newark's Palace Theatre is practically a haunted house with a stage. Its most famous spectral performer is a suicidal headmistress.

Apparently, a scandalous affair exposed within these very walls led her to a tragic end in the upper seating. Now, she makes unscheduled appearances, much to the surprise of staff and unsuspecting theatre-goers.

But she's not alone in the spotlight. This place is a veritable poltergeist playground. Dressing room doors slam, empty seats mysteriously lower, and props play hide-and-seek. And the disembodied footsteps and voices backstage? Just proof that some actors truly never leave the building.

What's a historic town without a haunted pub or two? The Old Kings Arms Public House is home to a rather boisterous character known affectionately as "Stomper." This unseen entity delights in opening and slamming doors and rearranging the furniture, all accompanied by a distinct, heavy stomping sound. He's probably just looking for the remote.

And for something truly peculiar, The former Ossington Coffee Tavern. Built as a temperance establishment, it's said that when alcohol was finally introduced to the premises around 1980, a portrait of Lady Ossington (the teetotal founder) would dramatically leap off the wall in protest. Now that's a spirit with strong convictions!

Other Documented/Reported Hauntings

Not all ghosts reside in grand, spooky locations. Sometimes, they just pop up in the most unexpected places. An intrepid cleaning lady at Barclay's Bank in Market Place once encountered a grey-haired woman in a long black dress, carrying towels, who promptly vanished through a solid door. Perhaps she was just looking for the staff room?

Even Morrisons Supermarket had a brief ghostly encounter in 2011, when a staff member spotted a phantom man in Victorian attire and a flat cap, affectionately dubbed "George," before he disappeared into a closed fridge door. Maybe he was just after a bargain on frozen peas.

Some hauntings aren't about specific spirits, but rather the lingering energy of past events. On Albert Street, a transparent man with a chain reportedly hobbles along, a chilling echo of a bygone era. And around Appleton Gate, the sounds of swords and horses occasionally cut through the night, a haunting soundtrack to Newark's Civil War past.

Even RAF Syerston has its own eerie mystery. One of its hangars is said to hold a presence that upsets guard dogs and causes sudden temperature drops. Given the intense history of military airfields, it's not hard to imagine residual energies lingering.

And just down the road at East Stoke, the location of "the Red Gutter" is said to be a hive of battlesounds on foggy evenings Further mentions

Newark Cemetery (Polish Section): Polish Airman: A man in uniform has been seen standing by headstones in the Polish section, believed to be the ghost of a Polish airman from WWII. Governor's House, Footsteps & Violets: In the 1990s footsteps were heard in the loft, and the strong scent of violets was often present.

Hanged Man of White Hart - This pub was said to be home to the ghost of a man hanged for a forgotten crime close by. Grey lady of the Woolpack (Now the prince rupert pub) - This phantom grey woman is said to haunt the bar area.

If these tales have piqued your interest (and perhaps given you a slight shiver down the spine), there are plenty of ways to delve deeper. Ian Gillanders' "Newark's Historical Ghost Walk" is an excellent starting point, providing even more chilling details and locations.

You can also join one of his many guided ghost walks that regularly happen in Newark.

www.newarkghostwalks.co.uk

This is just a glimpse into Newark's architectural heritage. **www.newarkguide.co.uk** includes everything from former maltings and breweries to telephone kiosks and war memorials.

Newark On Trent - A Sometimes Witty Journey Through Time

Ever wondered what happens when you mix mammoth hunters, Roman potters, Viking landlords, Civil War cannonballs, and a 21st-century bloke with a curious mind and a sarcasm problem? **You get this book!**

Written by local and self-declared "heritage whisperer" Dave Fargher, this is Newark-on-Trent's entire history—told with wit, warmth, and a healthy disrespect for dusty textbooks.

From flint tools to fibre broadband, this book takes you on a whirlwind tour through the town's prehistoric party pads, medieval mayhem, Tudor textiles, Victorian viaducts, and digital-age delights.

Who's it for?
History lovers who like their facts with a side of fun. .Locals who've walked past Newark Castle a thousand times and still don't know why King John died there (spoiler: it wasn't the food). Visitors who want to know what makes this market town tick (and occasionally explode).Anyone who thinks history should be more pub chat than PowerPoint.

Colette and the Watch of Time: Newark"

Join Colette, a girl with a magical pocket watch, as she tumbles through time to explore the amazing history of Newark-on-Trent! From dodging woolly mammoths in the Ice Age to building ancient henges, and from bustling Roman roads to the dramatic English Civil War, Colette experiences it all firsthand.

This isn't just history; it's a hilarious, whirlwind adventure through 14,000 years, bringing Newark's incredible past to life with every turn of her watch. Get ready for a fun-filled journey that proves history is anything but boring!

Perfect for curious kids (ages 7-12) who love adventure and magic, and for parents and educators looking for a fun way to bring history to life. It's also a charming read for anyone with a connection to Newark-on-Trent, eager to see their town's unique story unfold.

Newark On Trent Colouring Book

The Town By The River
Created By www.newarkguide.co.uk

Discover Newark-on-Trent like never before with this fun and educational colouring book!

Perfect for kids and curious minds of all ages, this beautifully designed book features **10 detailed illustrations of Newark's most iconic historic sites with descriptions** — ready for you to bring to life with colour,.

This book also features a **timeline** and **story of Newarks history.**

Whether you're a local or a visitor, this colouring book is a creative way to explore the heritage of Newark-on-Trent and learn while having fun!

A Special Creative Treat

Have fun!
:)

All pictures converted from Photos taken by Dave Fargher

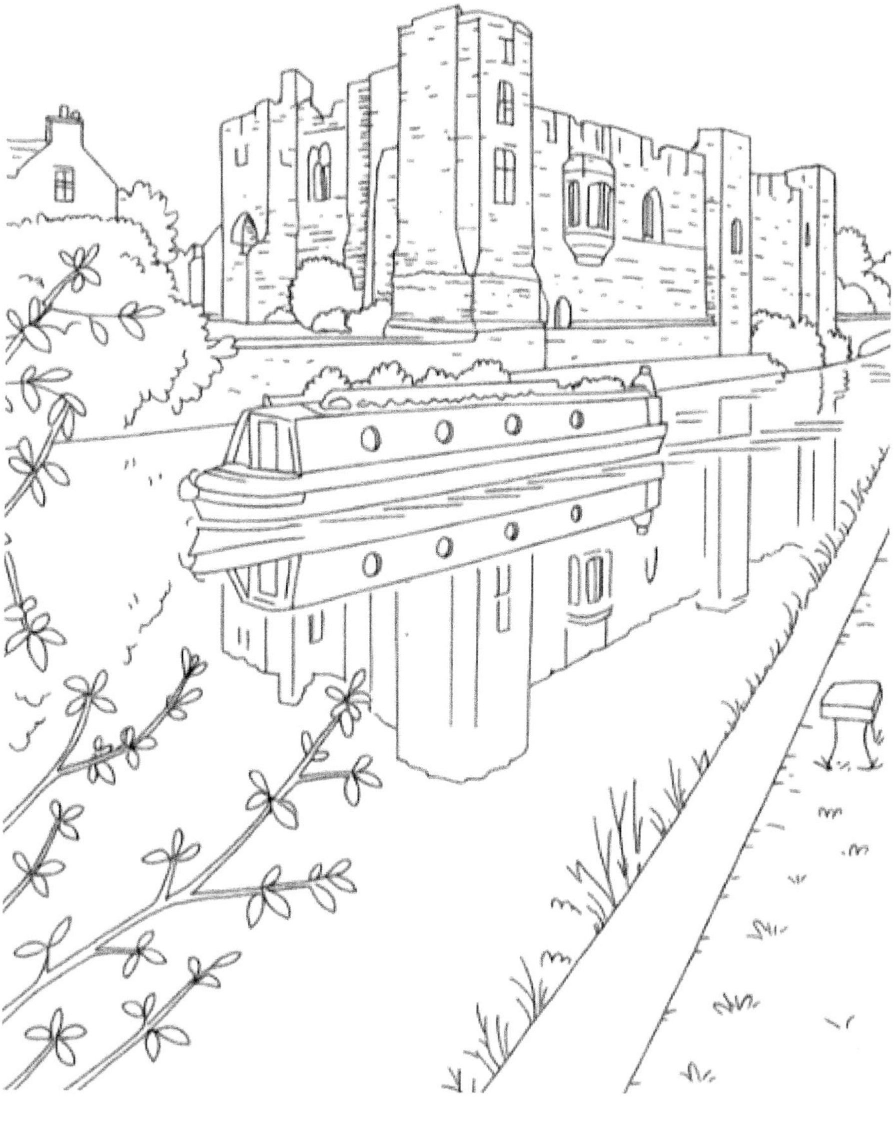

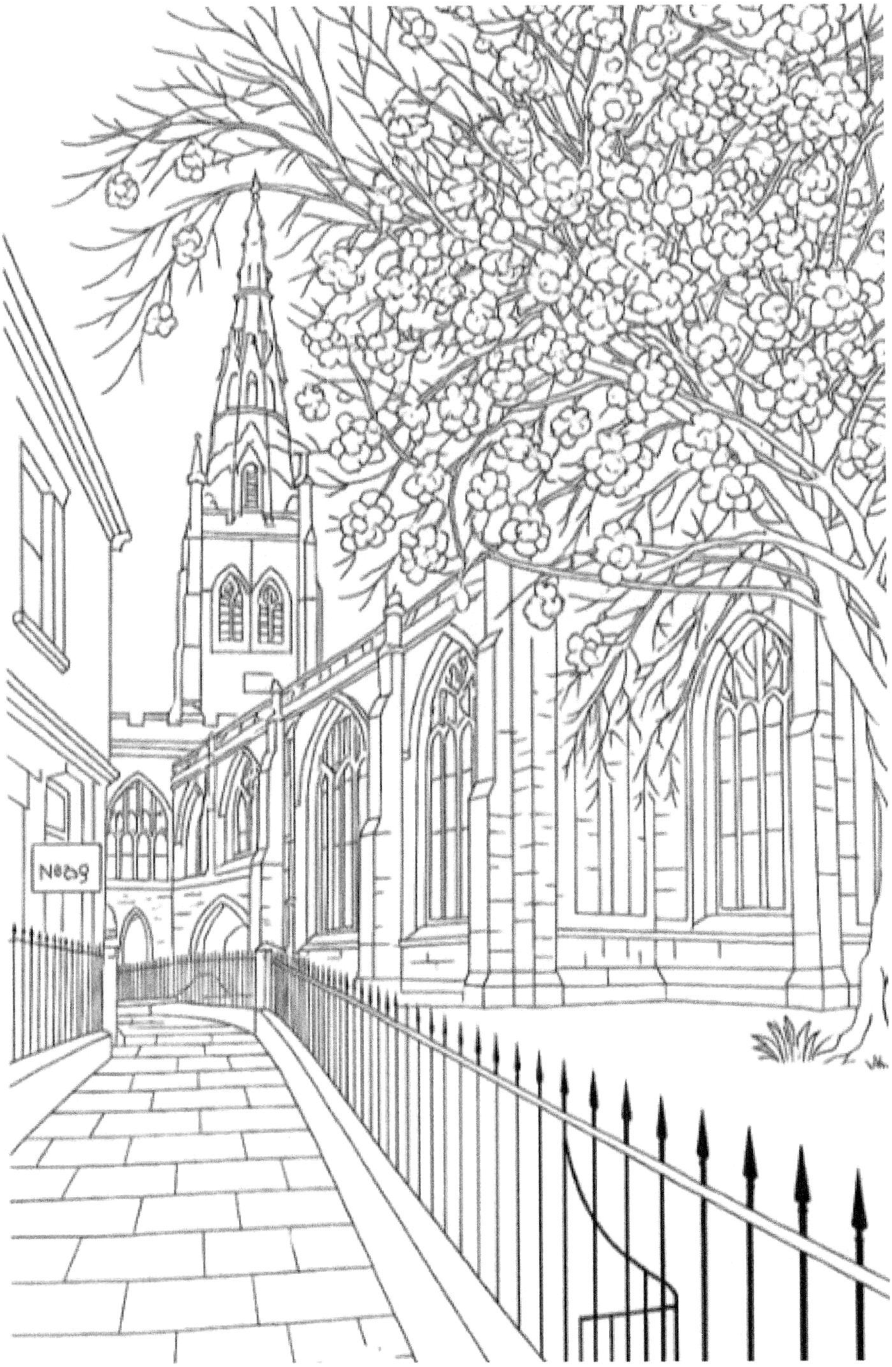

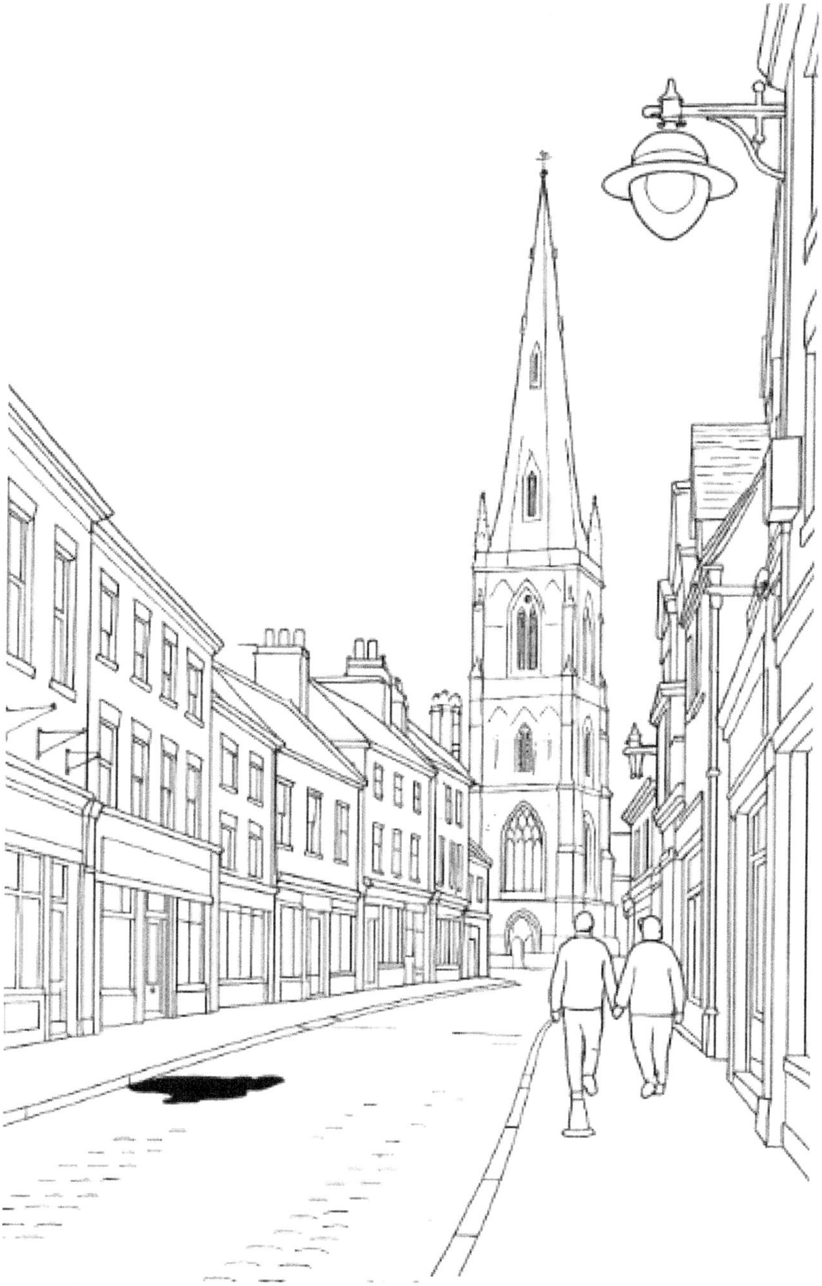

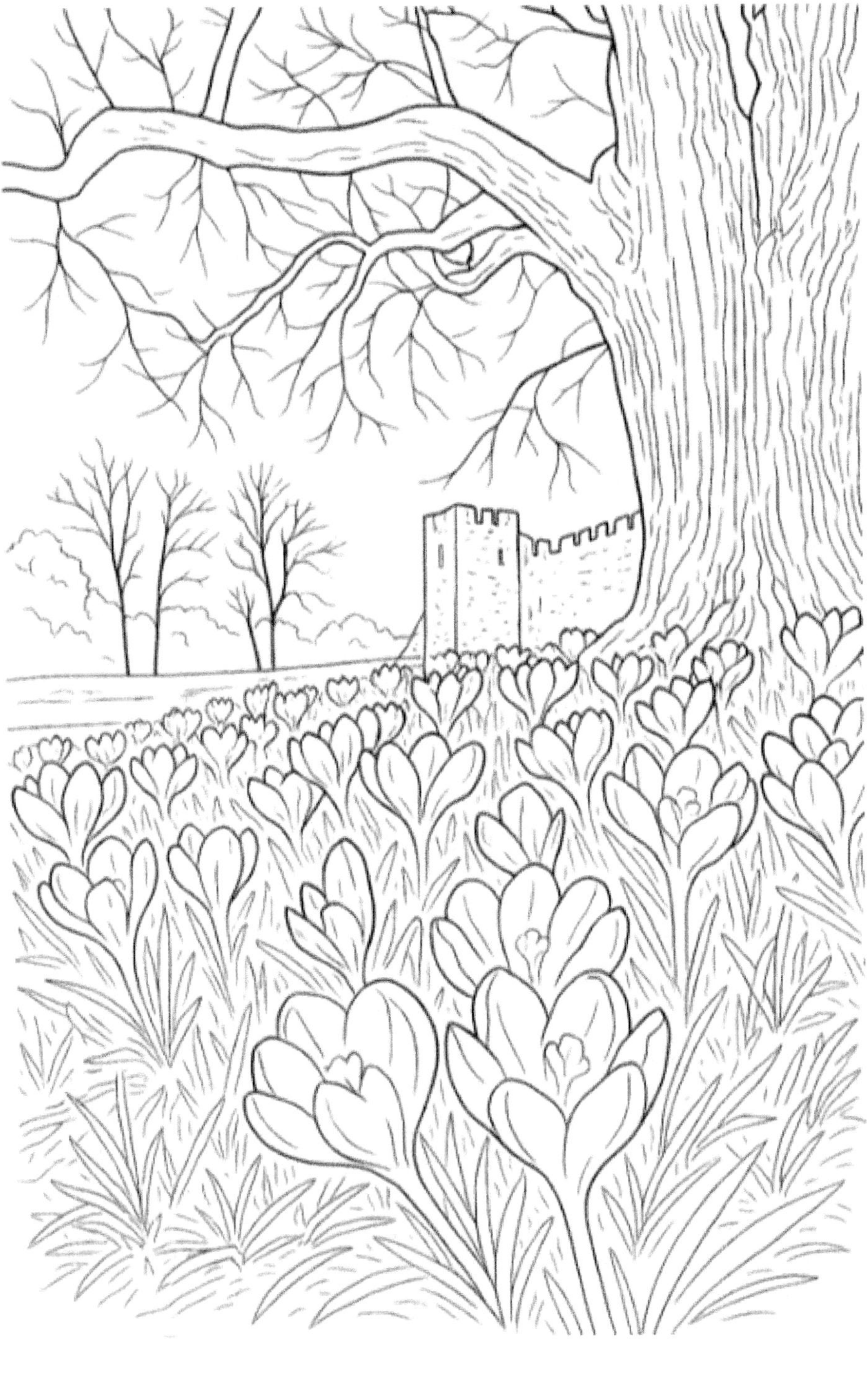

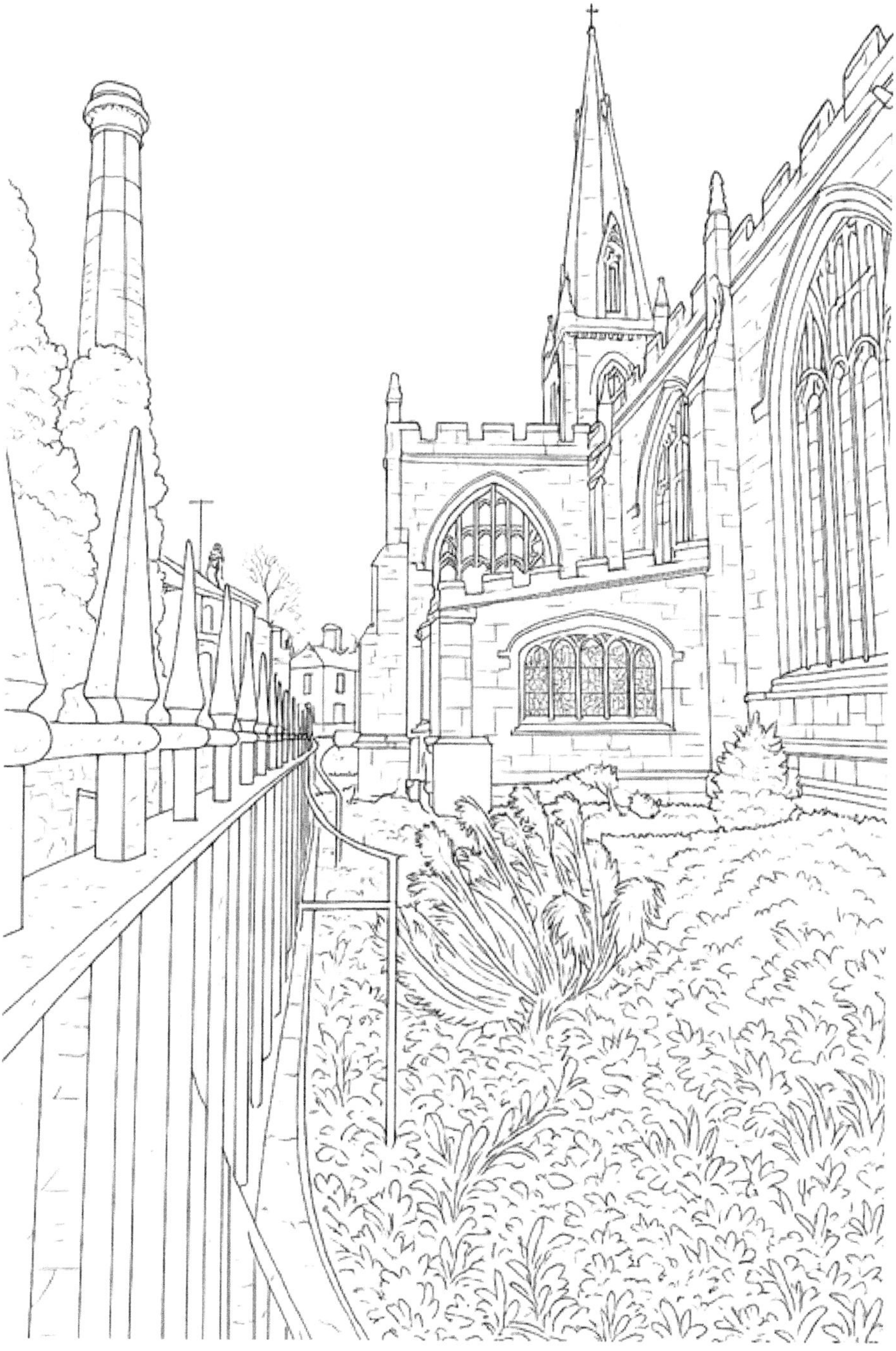

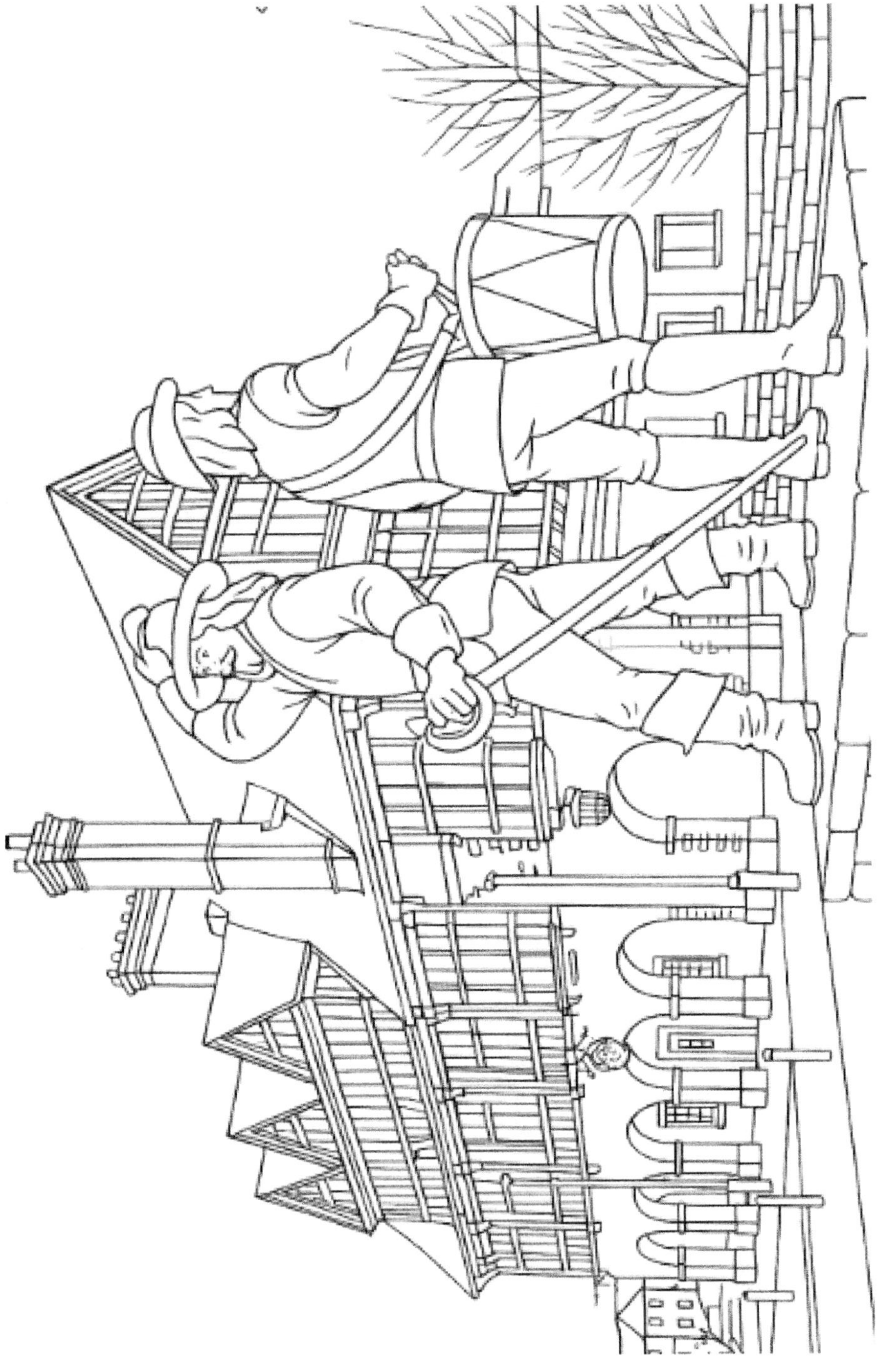

271

Designed and Created by Dave Fargher

Thanks.

WWW.NEWARKGUIDE.CO.UK

IMMERSE YOURSELF IN THE CAPTIVATING HISTORY OF NEWARK-ON-TRENT, NOTTINGHAMSHIRE.

WE ARE DEDICATED TO SHOWCASING THE LOCAL HISTORIC SITES, SHARING STORIES OF THE RESIDENTS, AND PRESERVING THE ESSENCE OF OUR TOWN'S PAST FOR GENERATIONS TO COME.

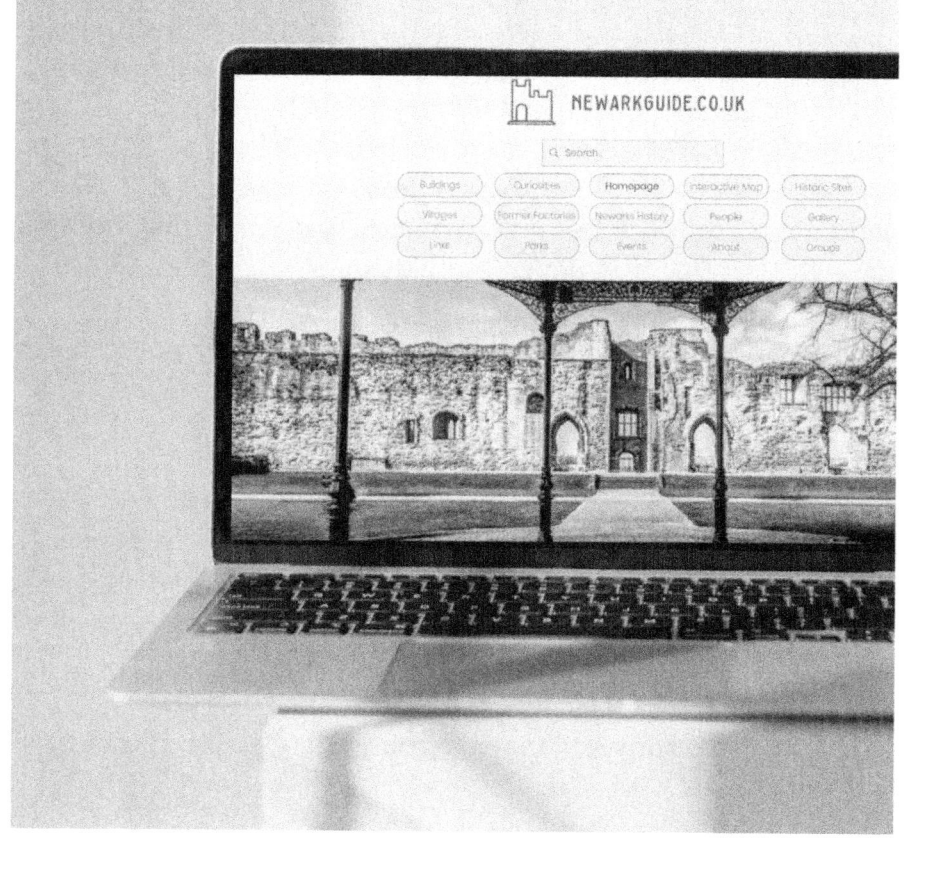

Free Guide to Newark on Trent

For anyone new or existing visiting the town, Newark Guide contains a wealth of information on Newark's fascinating history, from its pre-historic roots to its industrial heyday, Curiosities and sites, Events, groups and the people who have shaped the town and continue to do so.

Newark Guide – www.newarkguide.co.uk

Visitors can explore a treasure trove of information, including:

Historic Sites and buildings:
Discover the town's iconic landmarks, such as the imposing Newark Castle, and delve into their captivating histories, including once-thriving industries, factories, warehouses and the impact they had on its development.

Curiosities:
Find out more about lesser known sites and places that you may never know existed

A full history of Newark going back 14,000 years
The Myth of The Newark Tunnels
The Old town Walls
Town Trails

Interactive maps:
Navigate the town and surrounding areas with a free interactive maps.

Search function:
Simply search any key word to bring up related information

Local Legends:
Uncover fascinating tales of the people who have shaped

Newark's past, from renowned figures to artists, famous faces to everyday heroes.

Surrounding Villages:
Explore the charming villages that surround Newark, each with its own distinct history and character.

Also included:
Photo & Video gallery

Parks and public spaces
Useful links & Contact
Events around the town
Commmunity Groups
Useful Info about visiting

If you enjoy taking photos, please do share any of our beautiful town to Newark-on-Trent Photographs

Printed in Dunstable, United Kingdom